RESCUING THE DANISH JEWS

A Heroic Story From the Holocaust

Titles in
The Holocaust Through Primary Sources
Series:

AUSCHWITZ
Voices From the Death Camp
Library Ed. ISBN: 978-0-7660-3322-1
Paperback ISBN: 978-1-59845-346-1

KRISTALLNACHT
The Nazi Terror That Began the Holocaust
Library Ed. ISBN: 978-0-7660-3324-5
Paperback ISBN: 978-1-59845-345-4

LIBERATION
Stories of Survival From the Holocaust
Library Ed. ISBN: 978-0-7660-3319-1
Paperback ISBN: 978-1-59845-348-5

RESCUING THE DANISH JEWS
A Heroic Story From the Holocaust
Library Ed. ISBN: 978-0-7660-3321-4
Paperback ISBN: 978-1-59845-343-0

SAVING CHILDREN FROM THE HOLOCAUST
The Kindertransport
Library Ed. ISBN: 978-0-7660-3323-8
Paperback ISBN: 978-1-59845-344-7

THE WARSAW GHETTO UPRISING
Striking a Blow Against the Nazis
Library Ed. ISBN: 978-0-7660-3320-7
Paperback ISBN: 978-1-59845-347-8

RESCUING THE DANISH JEWS

A Heroic Story From the Holocaust

The Holocaust Through Primary Sources

Ann Byers

Enslow Publishers, Inc.
40 Industrial Road
Box 398
Berkeley Heights, NJ 07922
USA
http://www.enslow.com

Library of Congress Cataloging-in-Publication Data

Byers, Ann.
    Rescuing the Danish Jews : a heroic story from the Holocaust / Ann Byers.
        p. cm. — (The Holocaust through primary sources)
    Includes bibliographical references and index.
    Summary: "Examines the rescue of the Danish Jews during World War II, including background on
Denmark and the Holocaust, firsthand accounts from the many people involved, and how thousands of
Jews were saved from the Nazis"—Provided by publisher.
    ISBN 978-0-7660-3321-4
    1. Jews—Persecutions—Denmark—Juvenile literature. 2. Holocaust, Jewish
(1939–1945)—Denmark—Juvenile literature. 3. World War, 1939–1945—Jews—Rescue—Denmark—
Juvenile literature. 4. Denmark—History—German occupation, 1940–1945—Juvenile literature.
5. Denmark—Ethnic relations—Juvenile literature. I. Title.
DS135.D4B94 2011
940.53'183509489—dc22   2009053595

Paperback ISBN: 978-1-59845-343-0

Printed in China

10 9 8 7 6 5 4 3 2 1

052011 Leo Paper Group, Heshan City, Guangdong, China.

To Our Readers: We have done our best to make sure all Internet Addresses in this book were active and appropriate when we went to press. However, the author and the publisher have no control over and assume no liability for the material available on those Internet sites or on other Web sites they may link to. Any comments or suggestions can be sent by e-mail to comments@enslow.com or to the address on the back cover.

Every effort has been made to locate all copyright holders of material used in this book. If any errors or omissions have occurred, please contact us at www.enslow.com. We will try to make corrections in future editions.

Illustration Credits: Associated Press, pp. 42, 46, 111; Enslow Publishers, Inc., p. 56; The Granger Collection, New York, pp. 28, 75, 110; © Heritage-Images / The Image Works, p. 11; © From the Jewish Chronicle Archive / Heritage-Images / Imagestate, p. 99; The Museum of Danish Resistance 1940–1945, pp. 8, 32, 102, 103, 105; © Peter Horree / Alamy, p. 52; © Photothèque CICR (DR), pp. 87, 96; Public Domain Image, p. 25; © Shutterstock ®, p. 38; ullstein bild – dpa, p. 20; ullstein bild / The Granger Collection, New York, p. 61; USHMM, pp. 10, 50–51, 63; USHMM, courtesy of Edgar and Hana Krasa, p. 82; USHMM, courtesy of Ellis D. Gordon, p. 71; USHMM, courtesy of Frihedsmuseet, pp. 16, 24, 43, 48, 54, 66, 76, 90; USHMM, courtesy of Fritz Gluckstein, p. 83; USHMM, courtesy of Hanna Ben-Yami, p. 85; USHMM, courtesy of Leif Donde, p. 74; USHMM, courtesy of Leo Goldberger, pp. 17, 68, 70; USHMM, courtesy of Dr. Marvin Chadab, pp. 34–35; USHMM, courtesy of Museet for Danmarks Frihedskamp, p. 13; USHMM, courtesy of Scherl Bilderdienst, p. 33; USHMM, courtesy Swedish Red Cross, p. 92; USHMM, courtesy of YIVO Institute for Jewish Research, New York, p. 84.

Cover Illustration: USHMM, courtesy of Frihedsmuseet (Jewish refugees in Denmark board a ferry for Sweden in October 1943); USHMM, courtesy of Fritz Gluckstein (Star of David artifact).

Contents

INTRODUCTION

Denmark Is Different

The boat looked far too small. Bent Melchior was only fourteen years old, but he could tell the fishing vessel was built to hold five people at the most. There were six in his family alone, and others wanted to be on the boat, too. All of them were desperate to get out of Denmark. Just days before, the Germans had tried to arrest all the Jews in the country. Their only hope of safety was to get across the strait to Sweden. And so, at 7:00 that night, nineteen people squeezed aboard the little craft.

Melchior later remembered that the frightened Jews "lay in the boat like fish. This wasn't a boat meant for passengers. It was very cold, crowded and dirty."[1] But it was their only means of escape. He could put up with anything for the hour or two it would take to get to freedom.

But eleven hours later, the boat was still in the water, and Melchior knew that something was dreadfully wrong. Land was ahead, and a lighthouse beckoned, but the land was Denmark, and the lighthouse was manned by Germans. The inexperienced pilot had lost his way in the dark. "He was very frightened and almost out of fuel," Melchior said.[2] Melchior's father, Marcus, grabbed the wheel, turned the boat around, and sped away.

The Melchior family in Sweden after their turbulent journey from Denmark in October 1943. Marcus Melchior (left), Bent's father, took control of the fishing boat to guide it to safety in Sweden.

Just as the weary passengers spotted land, the engine sputtered. They had no more fuel. Within minutes, fishermen were rowing their boats toward the stranded refugees. Melchior heard the wonderful words, "Welcome to Sweden!"

★★★★★

Sweden was a safe harbor from the war that raged in Europe. The armies of Germany had barreled across Poland in 1939 and subdued France, Belgium, the Netherlands, Luxembourg, Norway, and Denmark in their *blitzkrieg*, or lightning war, in the spring of 1940. They had not attacked Sweden, which declared itself a neutral country, not taking sides in what was to become a bloody, global conflict.

When Germany invaded Denmark, the Nazis treated Denmark differently. Germany took control of the other nations right away, but not Denmark. German officials said they were there to "protect" Denmark; they let Denmark's government run the country. The rulers of the other nations fled, but King Christian X stayed in Denmark.

The situation with the Jews of Denmark was also different. In many other countries, antisemitism—prejudice against Jews—was strong, and people harassed and persecuted Jews long before the war. Jews often lived in their own neighborhoods, in segregated sections of cities. But Danish law forbade all racial and religious discrimination.[3] In Denmark, Jews lived among the other Danish people. As one citizen explained, "In Denmark we didn't distinguish between Jews and non-Jews, we were all just Danes."[4]

But Adolf Hitler, the German leader who started the Second World War, *did* distinguish between Jews and non-Jews. Beginning in 1933, he instituted a series of discriminatory actions against Jews. He stated plainly that he would use the war to rid Europe of all its Jews. This attempt later became known as the Holocaust. In the lands he conquered, Hitler ordered harsh measures against the Jews. They could not be on certain streets, their property was taken from them, and they had to wear a badge marking them as Jews. Within months, they were arrested, taken to camps, and eventually sent to their deaths. But not so in Denmark.

What made Denmark different from her neighbors? For one, Denmark barely fought the German invasion. The leaders of the little country knew they were no match for the armed might of Germany, so they gave up in less than two hours. They cooperated with the German occupiers, and Germany let Denmark keep its government and most of its freedoms.

Because Denmark was cooperative, Germany did not need to send brutal officials to keep people in line. Many of the soldiers assigned to Denmark were older men. They were not as radical about Nazism and the war as some of the younger soldiers. They were not concerned about moving up in their careers. Some closed their eyes when Danes disobeyed Nazi rules. As long as the government and King Christian cooperated, Germany had no reason to harm the Danes. Besides, Germany needed the food Denmark produced. If the Germans treated Denmark kindly, Denmark would supply them with fish, meat, and butter.

So for more than three years, from April 1940 to mid 1943, Denmark was peaceful. Guns, tanks, and sirens shook the rest of Europe, but Danes

Adolf Hitler issued harsh measures against Jews in all the territories he conquered. This photo of him was taken in 1933.

Evening Standard

Amusements 12
Radio 14

BLACK-OUT 8.15 pm, 5.48 am
MOON
Rose 7.4 am : Sets 9.38 pm

No. 36,066   LONDON, TUESDAY, APRIL 9, 1940   ONE PENNY

NORWAY AND DENMARK INVADED BY HITLER: FULL AID BY ALLIES

Copenhagen Occupied: 'Oslo Bombed'

NAZI TROOPS SHELLED AS THEY ATTEMPT TO LAND

THE British and French Governments are to extend full aid to Norway, following the invasion of Norway and Denmark by German troops to-day.

The British Foreign Office announced this afternoon that the necessary naval and military steps are being taken in conjunction with the French. They have informed Norway that they will fight the war in full association with them.

It is learned that the British statement refers only to Norway because it is impossible at the moment to say what the position is in Denmark, as all communications are cut off.

Paris radio (quoted in a New York message) reported that Norway formally asked for British and French aid.

GERMAN FORCES LANDED ON THE SOUTH COAST OF NORWAY AT 3 A.M., AND ARE REPORTED TO HAVE OCCUPIED A NUMBER OF TOWNS. DENMARK WAS INVADED AT 4.30 A.M. BY OVERWHELMING FORCES. THE GERMANS CLAIM THAT COPENHAGEN WAS IN THEIR HANDS BY 8 A.M.

A Reuter message from Malmo, Sweden, states that Denmark is entirely in German hands. Armed forces have occupied virtually all the important towns and military points.

OSLO WAS BOMBED FROM THE AIR SEVERAL TIMES, SAYS ASSOCIATED PRESS. IMMEDIATE EVACUATION WAS ORDERED. IT MUST BE COMPLETED BY TO-MORROW.

GERMAN AIRPLANES ALSO BOMBED CHRISTIANSAND, AT THE SOUTHERN TIP OF NORWAY. THE TOWN WAS EVACUATED AND COASTAL BATTERIES AT OAKARSBERG SHELLED GERMAN WARSHIPS WHICH WERE ATTEMPTING TO LAND TROOPS.

Oslo radio stated at 11 a.m. that four German warships were trying to get through the Oslo Fiord. One got through and then run aground in shallow water.

During the night warships which had tried to force an entry into the Oslo Fiord were repulsed by heavy fire from coastal batteries.

THE SWEDISH RADIO REPORTED THAT THE GERMANS

Admiral Sir Dudley Pound, the First Sea Lord, leaving Downing-street after to-day's Cabinet meeting.

THE ALLIES HAVE ASSURED NORWAY

THE following statement was issued by the British Foreign Office to-day:

"The German Government have issued a statement saying they have decided to take over the protection of Denmark and Norway.

"They add that this action is in reply to the laying of minefields in Norwegian territorial waters by Great Britain and France yesterday.

"Information has now reached H.M. Government to the effect that the German Minister at Oslo has demanded the surrender of Norway to Germany. In the event of refusal all resistance will be crushed.

"This demand was, of course, immediately refused by the Norwegian Government. Information has been received that German troops have already occupied Norwegian territory.

Will Deceive Nobody

"The German statement that their action is in reply to steps taken by the British and French Governments will deceive nobody. So elaborate an operation, involving simultaneous landings at a number of Norwegian ports by troops accompanied by naval forces, must have been planned long in advance.

"It is not surprising that the Norwegian Government have decided to resist this latest exhibition of German aggression.

"H.M. Government and the French Government have at once assured the German invasion of their country they have decided forthwith to extend their full aid to Norway and have intimated that they will fight the war in full association with them.

"The necessary naval and military steps are accordingly being taken in conjunction with the French."

Swiss Border Guard Doubled

TELEPHONE communication between Germany and Holland and Germany and Switzerland was broken off to-day.

Several hours later the telephone service between Amsterdam and Berlin was restored, says an Exchange message from Amsterdam.

Swiss guard along the frontiers was doubled this morning.

Reports about the concentration of German motorised units near the Dutch frontier are denied in Amsterdam, but since the outbreak of the war about 80 Nazi divisions have been permanently situated along the Dutch frontier. There are no signs

When Germany invaded Denmark, the Danish government surrendered without a fight. This front page of the *Evening Standard* newspaper from April 9, 1940, reports Germany's invasion of Denmark.

11

went about their business as usual. One boy, twelve at the time of the invasion, recalled:

> *Life went on as before, except that . . . they would post soldiers with guns and steel helmets and things like that in front of the banks and the hotels and important institutions that they wanted to guard. But besides that nothing happened really. . . . Life was continuing the way it was.*[5]

But that changed in 1943. By the summer, Germany was under attack from the Soviets in the east and the Allies in the west. Danes had begun to suffer from Germany's plunder of their land. Denmark's agricultural goods went to Germany while Danes went hungry. There were shortages of coal, gasoline, and other items. Some Danes began to look for ways to fight against the German occupiers. They blew up railroad tracks so that German forces could not use them. They set fire to trucks carrying supplies for German soldiers. Danish workers walked off their jobs in factories that were making products for Germany.

The growing sabotage angered the occupiers. The once-cooperative Danish government did not help to catch or punish the saboteurs. The Germans finally cracked down.

With all pretense of kindness to Denmark gone, Hitler turned his attention to Denmark's Jews. For three and a half years, while Jews all across the continent were being slaughtered, Denmark's

Danish fishermen (foreground) ferry Jews to Sweden in October 1943. More than seven thousand Jews were brought to Sweden aboard Danish boats.

7,500 Jews had been untouched (about 6,000 of the Jews living in Denmark were Danish citizens; the other 1,500 or so were refugees from other countries). But that would change. In Denmark, as in every other conquered nation, Jews would be arrested, transported to camps, and killed.

However, when word of the German plan leaked out, the Danes rose up as if to say, "This will not happen here!" Ordinary citizens hid their Jewish neighbors from German raids. When the hunt continued, those same citizens arranged to get the Jews out of the country. Sweden, only a few miles across the sea, was not controlled by Germany. In three weeks, the Danes ferried 7,200 Jews and 700 of their non-Jewish relatives to safety on three hundred fishing boats.

The Germans managed to arrest a small number of Jews in Denmark—fewer than five hundred. They were sent to a German concentration camp in Czechoslovakia. But even there, their countrymen sent them food, clothes, and medicine. The Danish government worked tirelessly to get them released. At the war's end, just over one hundred Danish Jews had died. Approximately 98 percent of Denmark's Jews were saved.

1 Sounding the Alarm: Georg Ferdinand Duckwitz

Sometimes heroes are good people who are in the right place at the right time. Such was Georg Duckwitz. He was a German businessman who had been living and working in Denmark on and off since 1929. His position made him a perfect link between German authority and the Danish citizens.

In the ten years before the German invasion, Duckwitz had made a number of contacts that would later prove very useful. When he worked for a shipping company, the Hamburg-Amerika Line, he befriended ship captains and harbor commanders. After war broke out, he worked for the *Abwehr*, the spy agency of the German army. This job gave him a thorough picture of the Danish political scene. He learned who the major players were, who held real power, and what side people were on. He made friends with many Danish people in positions of influence. After Germany invaded Denmark, Duckwitz was appointed an attaché, which meant he was "attached" to the German diplomatic office in Denmark. He was in charge of all shipping for Germany in the area. In this position, he would rub shoulders with the high-ranking Germans who had come to Denmark to "protect" it.

The most important of those Germans was Werner Best, who had helped develop the Gestapo—the ruthless Nazi police.

15

Georg Ferdinand Duckwitz

He had served Hitler in a number of high-level jobs. In November 1942, Hitler appointed Best plenipotentiary—his point person—in Denmark. His job was to stop the rising sabotage there and keep the government cooperating with Germany. He had to preserve the image of Denmark as a content "model protectorate." And he had to keep the food and manufactured goods of Denmark coming into Germany.

To accomplish this, Best needed to get to know Danish people. Who better to introduce him than his shipping attaché? Duckwitz had social as well as business contacts, and he was a long-time member of the Nazi Party. So Best cultivated a friendship with Duckwitz, which put the attaché in the right place.

The Crisis

Best's biggest problem was the Danish resistance, also called the underground. The resistance consisted of Danes unhappy with their government's cooperation with Germany. They had decided that if their leaders would not fight the occupation, they would.

THE THANK-YOU NOTE THAT TRIGGERED A CRISIS

On September 26, 1942, King Christian X of Denmark celebrated his seventy-second birthday. One of the people to wish him well was Adolf Hitler.

At that point in time, Germany had occupied Denmark for two and a half years. The king was still on his throne, and he still had some of his authority. But German soldiers and diplomats were the real power in his land; they took and did whatever they wanted. Hitler may have thought of Christian as an ally, but the king did not consider Hitler his friend.

Nevertheless, Hitler sent a birthday telegram to the king. It was a long note, with all the flowery praise people sometimes use on special occasions. Christian, being well-bred, sent a thank-you telegram. It said simply, *"Meinen besten Dank. Chr. Rex"* ("My utmost thanks. King Christian").

The short, formal reply infuriated Hitler. He immediately made Denmark's ambassador leave Germany. He removed Germany's ambassador in Denmark and sent in his place someone he hoped would be tougher (Werner Best). He replaced his military commander in Denmark. He demanded that the Danish prime minister resign and a new one be selected.

This diplomatic frenzy became known as the *Telegram Crisis*. Hitler's actions made it clear that Germany would maintain control of Denmark. But they also showed that superior force is not the only form of power.

King Christian X was ruler of Denmark during World War II. His short reply to Hitler's birthday telegram set in motion the placement of Werner Best as ambassador.

Their small acts of defiance grew in size and number, and they began to hurt Germany.

The resistance spread beyond the little bands of saboteurs. In the shipyards, Danes had jobs repairing German ships. When one of those ships was sabotaged, German soldiers arrested the saboteurs. In turn, the dockworkers walked off their jobs. The strike spread to factories, warehouses, and shops in that city and nearby towns. This made Best nervous.

The final straw was a massive bombing of a famous building. The Forum was the largest, grandest exhibition hall in all of Scandinavia. The Germans wanted the Danes to convert it into barracks for German soldiers. One day, when all the Danes working on the project left for lunch, a thunderous explosion reduced the cement structure to rubble.

Four days later, on August 28, 1943, Best made new demands of the Danish government, including sanctioning German military courts to prosecute saboteurs. Rather than agree, the Danish government resigned. Germany immediately declared a state of military emergency in Denmark, taking control of the Danish military and police forces. German officials arrested a number of people, and the king became a prisoner in his castle. Cooperation was officially over.

This turn of events was a personal blow to Best. As a diplomat, he no longer remained in charge; the commander of the army called the shots. Best tried to figure out how to regain his power. What could he do to convince Hitler that he was the right man to rule in Denmark? What was really important to Hitler? Best knew the answer: the annihilation of the Jews.

The Plan

Best sent a telegram to his superiors in Berlin, Germany. It read, in part:

> I hereby beg, in light of the new situation, to report on the Jewish problem in Denmark. . . . It is my opinion that measures should now be taken toward a solution of the problems of the Jews . . . as long as the present state of emergency exists, for afterward they will be liable to cause reaction in the country. . . . In order to arrest and deport some 6,000 Jews (including women and children) at one sweep it is necessary to have the [50 additional] police forces I requested. . . . Supplementary forces should be provided by the German military commander in Denmark. For transportation, ships must be considered a prime necessity and should be ordered in time.[1]

One of the first people Best consulted was Georg Duckwitz. As head of shipping, the attaché would need to coordinate the transport of Jews out of Denmark. Many historians believe Best

Hitler appointed Werner Best to keep the Danish government cooperating with Germany. Best struggled to stop the Danish resistance.

contacted Duckwitz to purposely leak the information about the upcoming raid. On one hand, Best needed to remain in the good graces of his German superiors. On the other hand, he wanted to stay in Copenhagen, so he did not want to upset the Danes.

Whatever Best's motives were, he informed Duckwitz of the impending action. Duckwitz did everything he could to stop the plan, including flying to Berlin to intercept the telegram before it reached Hitler. But he arrived too late. Hitler had already seen and approved Best's request. Denmark's Jews, like millions in other European nations, would be captured, shipped out of the country, and never heard from again. All that remained was to work out the details.

One important detail was identifying Jews. They did not look different from other Danes. They had never been required to register. How would they all be found? The answer was that many belonged to a Jewish Community Center, where they gathered for cultural and traditional events. The center in Copenhagen would have the names and addresses of all its members. Danish Nazis could supply the names of Jews that were not on the rolls of the center. The day Hitler's approval for the deportation came, the offices of the Jewish Community Center were broken into.

When Duckwitz heard this, he knew the *Aktion*, as the Nazis called their raids, could not be far off. He flew to neutral Sweden to persuade the prime minister to take in Denmark's Jews until the war ended. But he was unsuccessful. Sweden would take Denmark's Jews only if Germany would agree, and Germany would never agree.

By the time Duckwitz returned to Denmark, the additional Gestapo had already arrived. The boat that would carry the Jews away was steaming toward Copenhagen's harbor. The only remaining detail was the exact date of the raid.

The Warning

Duckwitz could do nothing to stop the planned *Aktion*. But he could at least blunt its impact. He would try to convince his Jewish friends to escape to Sweden. Using his contacts at the Swedish embassy, he obtained visas for several people that allowed them to leave Denmark legally.

But thousands more were still in mortal danger. If they tried to flee, surely the German navy patrolling the harbors would catch them. Duckwitz, however, knew the man in charge of those patrols. The two had worked together for the Hamburg-Amerika Line. He was German, but he did not like the idea of hunting down civilians. When Duckwitz explained the Nazis' plan, the harbor commander pretended to find problems with all his patrol boats. He took them out of commission for repairs. When the Jews actually made their escape, the patrol boats were docked. Ten years later, Duckwitz praised the harbor commander for his bravery:

> It is a tribute to the German Navy that I succeeded to at least lessen the dreadful consequences of the planned action, since I could no longer prevent it. I reasoned that the police forces would not be able to patrol the Danish coast on land and sea to stop any illegal crossings. The danger that German naval units would have to take over this job was prevented by the German harbor commander of Copenhagen. He saw to it that the coast guard ships were out of action. He took a great personal risk, but he did so without hesitation.[2]

On September 28, 1943, Best called his shipping attaché to his office. The *Aktion*, he told him, was three days away. It would take place the night of October 1.

Duckwitz had to get word to the Jews. Who would have the contacts among Jews? Who could he trust with the information? Who would act quickly enough? He thought of Hans Hedtoft, chairman of Denmark's largest political party. Hedtoft described what happened that night:

> [Duckwitz] came to see me while I was in a meeting. . . . "Now the disaster is about to occur," he said. "The whole thing is planned in full detail. Ships are going to anchor in the harbor of Copenhagen. Your poor Jewish fellow countrymen who will be found by the Gestapo will be forcibly transported to the ships and deported to an unknown fate." His face was white with indignation and shame. . . . I became speechless with rage and anxiety. This was too diabolic. I just managed to say, "Thank you for the news," and Duckwitz disappeared. He personally did everything that was possible to save as many human lives as he could.[3]

Duckwitz sounded the alarm, and others took over from there. The message got to Marcus Melchior, Bent's father and the active rabbi of the synagogue in Copenhagen. The next day was the eve of Rosh Hashanah, the Jewish New Year. The approaching holy day drew more than the usual number of Jews to the early morning service in the synagogue. When they arrived, Melchior stunned them with the news. He begged them to tell everyone

Marcus Melchior rides his bicycle in Copenhagen. Melchior was chief rabbi of the synagogue in Copenhagen during the Nazi occupation.

they knew and to find places to hide. Then he canceled the services and followed his own advice.

When the Gestapo conducted their raid, they found only 202 Jews.[4] The rest were in the basements, attics, and bedrooms of their non-Jewish neighbors, friends, and strangers. The Gestapo searched for days, but they arrested fewer than five hundred in all. Duckwitz's warning, as well as the kindness of their fellow Danes, saved them.

After the War

For the rest of the war, Duckwitz maintained his friendships with both the Germans and the Danes. However, when the British liberated Denmark, they arrested Duckwitz along with other German officials. In a matter of hours, Duckwitz's Danish friends spoke up for him and he was released. The Danes invited Duckwitz to stay in Denmark, but he felt a duty to help Germany recover from the scars of Nazism.

Georg Duckwitz received the Cross of the Commander of the Dannebrog Order from King Frederik IX, son of King Christian X.

Until his death in 1973, at the age of sixty-eight, Duckwitz served Germany in a number of positions, including ambassador to Denmark. In Denmark, King Frederik IX, son of wartime King Christian X, awarded him the Cross of the Commander of the Dannebrog Order. In Jerusalem, Duckwitz was named one of the *Righteous Among the Nations*, an honor reserved for non-Jews who rescued Jews during the Holocaust at great risk to their own lives.

Hiding Strangers:
Dr. Karl Henrik Køster

L ike Duckwitz, Karl Køster, a non-Jewish doctor, was in the right place at the right time. He was a surgeon at Bispebjerg Hospital, the largest medical facility in Copenhagen.

Dr. Køster happened to be in his apartment on the hospital grounds one night when a bleeding man came to his door. The man had been shot in the stomach at close range. He was a member of the resistance. German soldiers had caught his group as it was blowing up a factory. The soldiers thought they had killed him.

Køster did not argue with himself about whether he should help a saboteur. He rushed the man directly to the operating room. After he removed the bullets, he discovered that the man was also suffering from an ulcer. So, on his patient's medical chart he wrote as the diagnosis "perforated ulcer." After all, two bullets *had* punctured an ulcer. If the Germans were to check, they would find no record of anyone at the hospital that night with "gunshot wounds." Dr. Køster was in the right place to help the Danish resistance.

The First Jewish Refugees

He was also in the right place to help the Jews when the time came. That day arrived on October 7, 1943, less than a week

The Gestapo rounds up Danish Jews in Copenhagen in October 1943. Karl Køster helped hide Jews in his hospital so they were not captured by the Nazis.

after the German *Aktion*. After the raid, Jews were desperately trying to get to Sweden. Until they could safely make it to the coast, they remained in hiding. And the Germans kept looking for them. Some of the medical students on the hospital staff had been actively engaged in helping Jews escape. They had arranged transportation to the seacoast. They had found safe houses on the coast and fishing boats. But getting them out of the city was hard. Germans had been ordered to arrest Jews and anyone caught helping them. The students asked Køster if forty Jews could hide at the hospital. They would need only a few hours, until the trucks taking them to the coast could pick them up.

The hospital was huge, with several medical buildings as well as housing for most of the staff. It had a cemetery, a chapel, and a lovely garden. Certainly forty people could be hidden easily at Bispebjerg. But Køster wondered how forty Jews would get to the hospital without being seen by the Germans.

The students already had an answer. They told the Jews to look like they were going to a funeral. Funerals in Copenhagen were often followed by processions to the cemetery. The refugees would follow the hearse, dressed in black and carrying flowers. Forty people would not be an unusual number at a funeral. Neither would it be uncommon for children to be in a funeral procession. The students had the cars, the black clothes, and the flowers ready. Dr. Køster gave his okay.

More Refugees

The act went off as planned with one small problem. Instead of forty Jews, one hundred forty came for the funeral! Only forty could be taken to the coast that day. The rest would have to wait. That meant keeping them at the hospital at least overnight, maybe longer. It meant feeding them and finding them passage to the coast. It meant trouble for the hospital if they were discovered. Even so, Køster did not hesitate. He found room for the hundred unexpected Jews in the hospital's psychiatric building.

But that hundred and forty was just the beginning. The next morning, two hundred more Jews arrived at the hospital. No one at the hospital knew they were coming. No one had prepared for their exit to Sweden. Somehow the Jews in hiding had heard that

Bispebjerg was a safe place and that a doctor there would help them escape.

But there was no more room in the psychiatric building. Where would Køster put them? He thought of the nurses who lived in apartments in the hospital complex. Without hesitation, the nurses made arrangements to house the Jews in their rooms. The head nurse, Signe Jansen, spoke for all the nurses when she explained why:

> *I was brought up to believe in democracy and to believe that you have to be willing to fight if you want to preserve that democracy. As for helping the Jews, . . . I never thought of them as Jews or anything else. They were merely my countrymen and they needed my help.[1]*

The large number of Jewish refugees created another problem the medical students had not anticipated. How would they get so many to the waiting fishing boats? Again, Køster was in the right place. He had a fleet of ambulances at his disposal. Ambulances could hold several people. They could travel without suspicion any time of day or night. The Germans were not likely to check them out.

Word of Bispebjerg's rescue operation spread. Doctors and medical students involved in the resistance were among those who carried the news. For them, helping Jews escape was not only the kind thing to do, but it was also a way of defying Germany. One medical student, Robert Pedersen, described what he did:

> I went from house to house. . . . Whenever I saw a name plate that indicated a Jewish family, I rang the doorbell and asked to talk to them. Sometimes they did not believe me. But I succeeded in persuading them to pack and come with me to Bispebjerg Hospital. . . . I merely turned them over to the receptionist. After that the doctors and nurses took care of them. And then I went back to my neighborhood and collected more Jews.[2]

Nearly everyone on staff at Bispebjerg was involved in the rescue, from surgeons to gatekeepers to kitchen crew. While the hospital maintained normal operation, one hundred thirty nurses cared for the refugees in their apartments. Other hospitals became part of the effort, and many doctors joined in. People from all over the country sent money to the hospitals to help with expenses. In all, about two thousand Jews were saved through the hospitals.[3]

Dangerous Work

Every one of the hundreds of Danes involved in the undertaking took part at great risk. Eventually, the Germans began raiding the Bispebjerg Hospital, looking for Jews. On one of those searches,

THE CHURCHILL CLUB

The earliest known organized resistance to the German occupation of Denmark was the *Churchill-Klubben* (Churchill Club)—a group of eleven teenage boys. Two brothers, Knud and Jens Pedersen, started the club. Its purpose was to keep the Germans from winning in Denmark. Their slogan was: "If the adults won't do something, we will!"

Members of the Churchill Club stand in line for a photo after their arrest in May 1942. The group of teenage boys committed many acts of sabotage against the Nazis.

They did quite a bit for a small collection of schoolboys. They committed twenty-five acts of sabotage. Their "best job was the burning of a freight train loaded with war materials."[4]

The acts were small, but each one frustrated and hindered the Germans. The boys hoped that Churchill's soldiers—the British—would free their country. When that happened, they would join the British with their own weapons. They got their weapons by stealing them from German soldiers:

While a couple of us engaged [the soldiers] in friendly conversation, the others would steal the rifles they propped against a wall or bench. Our best hunting grounds were the restaurants. The German officers hung their belts and holsters in the cloakrooms and we would pinch the pistols from them. The local barracks was another good spot. . . . While they were in their huts, polishing their equipment or busy with other chores, we'd lift their rifles through the open windows.[5]

The stealing, not the sabotage, became their undoing. They were caught, tried, and convicted. One thirteen-year-old was freed, but the others received prison sentences ranging from one and a half to three years. Even in prison, they resisted. They escaped at night and continued to sabotage German interests.

they found a doctor operating on a Jewish patient. They killed the doctor, the patient, and the nurses assisting with the surgery.[6]

The threat of death did not stop Dr. Køster from helping with the rescue of Jews. At times, he personally escorted the fleeing families to the boats. Once he traveled about forty miles with more than one hundred fifty refugees in fifty taxis. The group was spotted on the beach by a German patrol. The Jews and Køster dove for the taxis and the vehicles sped to another port. There Køster bought a boat and put all one hundred fifty people on it. The extra trip cost the doctor more than $22,000.[7]

More than six thousand Danish Nazis listen to an address during an assembly on May 19, 1942. These Nazis would help the Gestapo track down people trying to help the Jews escape. Nazi agents came after Karl Køster.

It was simply a matter of time before the Germans began to suspect Køster. The Gestapo came to his apartment, but he was not there. When he was a short distance from his home, he watched the Nazi agents shoot a medical student in the back, killing him on the street. He knew he had been discovered. Køster, who had smuggled thousands of Jews to Sweden, also escaped on a boat to Sweden.

After the Rescue

In helping the Jews, Køster had become part of the Danish resistance. He was not content to remain safe in neutral Sweden. He wanted to continue the fight against Nazi Germany. He went to the British Embassy in Stockholm, Sweden, and offered his services to the British army. He was a surgeon, and an army in wartime could always use good doctors.

After escaping to Sweden, Karl Køster became a medical officer for the British army. He was part of a unit that liberated the Nazi camp Bergen-Belsen. In this photo, American soldiers view the bodies of prisoners laid out in rows at the Ohrdruf camp in Germany, after it was liberated on April 4, 1945.

The British gladly accepted Køster's offer. For the next three years, he served as a medical officer. He did not encounter Jews in large numbers again until April 1945. He was part of the British unit that liberated the German concentration camp at Bergen-Belsen. He saw with his own eyes the horrible atrocities the Nazis committed against the Jews. He was grateful to have helped keep some from that fate.

When the war ended, Køster returned to Denmark. He learned that his wife had spent five weeks in German prisons but had not given up any information.

When the doctor was asked why he did what he did, he said, "It was the natural thing to do. I would have helped any group of Danes being persecuted. The Germans' picking on the Jews made as much sense to me as picking on redheads."[8]

3 Finding a Safe Place: Niels Bohr

Duckwitz and Køster made major contributions to the rescue because they were in the right place. Niels Bohr was the right person.

His father was a physiology professor at the University of Copenhagen. Bohr followed in his scientific father's footsteps. By the time he earned his doctorate in 1911, he was already known for his brilliant mind. He became the first person to describe the structure of the atom. For this, he was awarded the Nobel Prize in Physics in 1922.

Bohr not only described the atom, but he discovered how to manipulate it to produce nuclear energy. He wanted to harness that energy for peaceful purposes, but other people had different ideas. During World War II, both Germany and the Allies saw the potential of the atom as a weapon. Both wanted to make an atom bomb. And both knew that the person most likely to figure out how to make it was Niels Bohr.

Before the war, Bohr was the head of the Institute for Theoretical Physics (later renamed for Bohr) at the University of Copenhagen. This was a school and laboratory devoted to the study of the new field of nuclear science. Bohr invited people from all over the world to study there. He wanted scientists to share their discoveries and their theories with one another.

A view of the University of Copenhagen today. Niels Bohr invited Jewish scientists who had been driven out of Germany and other nations to study at his Institute for Theoretical Physics at the University of Copenhagen.

He felt that having many physicists in one place would push all of them to greater heights. And it did. At least five other men who studied at the university received Nobel Prizes, including Bohr's son Aage.[1] When Jewish scientists were driven out of Germany and other countries, Bohr welcomed them at his institute.

A Wanted Man

One of those who studied in Copenhagen before the war was a German, Werner Heisenberg. Like Bohr, Heisenberg, a brilliant physicist, received a Nobel Prize for his research. As Bohr did with all his students, he developed a friendship with the German. In the fall of 1941, Heisenberg and another German paid Bohr a visit. Years later, Bohr wrote about the meeting:

> Through the German authorities Heisenberg and Weizsäcker had arranged a physics conference at the German Institute in Copenhagen, which had been established by the occupying power. Only a few Danes took [part] in this conference, and among them none of the leading physicists at the University's Institute for Theoretical Physics.[2]

Bohr remembered clearly that neither he nor any of his friends participated in the conference set up by the German scientists. Bohr was outspoken in his criticism of Nazi Germany. He had even donated his Nobel Prize to the war effort in neighboring Finland. His institute was a refuge for Jewish scientists fleeing from Germany. Still, he did agree to see Heisenberg. After all, they had been friends:

> *During a conversation . . . Heisenberg stated that he was working on the release of atomic energy and expressed his conviction that the war, if it did not end with a German victory, would be decided by such means [that is, an atomic bomb].*[3]

This was Heisenberg's hint to Bohr that Germany was trying to build an atomic bomb. Bohr knew that such a powerful weapon was theoretically possible. He thought, however, that making a bomb would take many years. He did not know that his former student was the lead scientist in a German program attempting to build the weapon. Heisenberg's revelation not only stunned him; it worried him. He "restrained himself from any comment but understood that this was important information which he was obliged to try to bring to the attention of the English."[4]

Bohr did not know that the English, as well as the Americans, were already trying to build atomic bombs. Since the German occupation, Denmark's scientists had been isolated from the rest of the world. But people in Germany knew. The Allies and the Germans were in a race to be first with a nuclear weapon. If Niels Bohr were to help the Allies, the Allies would win.

The Allies desperately wanted Bohr. At the beginning of 1943, the British government sent secret messages to Bohr. The British would find a way to get him out of the country. Would he come to England and work on the Allies' atomic bomb project? Bohr did not believe a nuclear bomb was a very realistic possibility. He responded that he needed to stay in Denmark to defend his institute and

> those scientists in exile who have sought refuge here. But neither such duties nor even the danger of retaliation against my colleagues and family would have sufficient weight to hold me here, if I felt that I could be of any real help . . . though this is hardly probable. I feel convinced, in spite of any future prospects, that any immediate use of the latest marvelous discoveries of atomic physics is impractical.[5]

The Germans, however, not only believed the bomb was practical, but they were working feverishly to make it a reality. They could not let Bohr work for the other side.

Escape

The Germans decided to arrest Bohr at about the same time they decided to deport the Jews. By happy coincidence for them, Bohr was a Jew. He had never practiced Judaism, but his mother's parents

Niels Bohr at his desk in 1933. Bohr became an important man in the race to build an atomic bomb.

were Jewish. And that, by Nazi definition, made him Jewish. The Nazis classified as Jewish anyone with one Jewish parent or three Jewish grandparents; a person like Bohr, with two Jewish grandparents, was a *Mischlinge*, a half Jew. Bohr would be arrested with everyone else in the Rosh Hashanah raid.

Bohr learned of the threat to his life very early on September 29. He had just a few hours to make his escape. He packed only one bag so he would not arouse suspicion. Because Denmark was under martial law, no one could be out at night. So, leaving his home during the day with his wife and sons, he made his way to the coast. Members of the Danish resistance, who had been working with the British, took them to a house where they could wait for dark. The underground arranged for two fishing boats: one for him and a later one for the rest of his family. On September 30, a day before the scheduled raid, Bohr was in Sweden.

Even though he was out of reach of the Gestapo, Bohr was not safe. The Germans had learned of his escape, and they dispatched their agents in Sweden to find him. They could not let him get to England or America. They would kill him first, if they had to. Bohr could not wait for his family. Members of the resistance whisked him by train from the seaside town of Limhamn to the capital of Stockholm. There, the British were waiting to take him to England.

Safety for Others

But Bohr was not ready to go. He thought about the Nazi raid about to happen in Denmark. Thousands of Jews had no place of safety. Sweden had not agreed to shelter them. Perhaps he could

This view from a Danish fishing boat shows another one ahead of it. Both boats were carrying Danish Jews to safety in Sweden. On September 29, 1943, Niels Bohr escaped to Sweden aboard a fishing boat.

use his own importance to convince the Swedish government to take in Denmark's Jews.

Bohr took his request all the way to the king. He asked for more than sanctuary for the Jews. He also wanted Sweden to make that offer public so the Jews in Denmark would know about it. King Gustav agreed. Within days of Bohr's arrival, Sweden's newspapers carried the offer on their front pages. Swedish radio broadcast the news into Denmark. The Jews who were in hiding throughout Denmark knew that if they could make it to Sweden, they would be safe.

Bohr was now happy to leave. His son Aage would follow him to London, and the rest of his family would stay in Sweden until the war ended. Bohr was flown on a military plane called a Mosquito bomber. The bomb bay of the plane had been modified to hold a passenger instead of a bomb. The flight would be uncomfortable, but German radar would have a hard time spotting the small wooden plane.

The pilot gave Bohr a helmet with earphones and an oxygen mask. The pilot would climb to 20,000 feet and radio the scientist to put the oxygen mask on. He would need the oxygen at the high altitude. But Bohr's large head did not fit properly in the helmet. The earphones were too high for him to hear the pilot's message. Without oxygen, Bohr fainted as the air thinned. The frantic pilot kept trying to radio Bohr, but the physicist did not respond. The pilot dove to a lower altitude, saving Bohr's life.

A Safer World

On October 8, the *New York Times* reported Bohr's safe arrival in England. The newspaper also hinted at what the scientist would do next:

> Dr. Niels H. D. Bohr, refugee Danish scientist and Nobel Prize winner for atomic research, reached London from Sweden today bearing what a Dane in Stockholm said were plans for a new invention involving atomic explosions.
>
> The plans were described as of the greatest importance to the Allied war effort.[6]

Bohr was shocked to learn of the progress the Allies had made toward creating an atomic bomb. Building the weapon was indeed practical. The fact that something so powerful was actually possible raised a larger question. Would making a nuclear bomb start an arms race that would keep countries fighting each other? The question haunted Bohr, and he later wrote: "Humanity will, therefore, be confronted with dangers of unprecedented character unless . . . measures can be taken to forestall a disastrous competition in such formidable armaments."[7]

Bohr decided that an atomic bomb could end "the great menaces of oppression to so many peoples" and bring "an immense relief . . . all over the world," and afterward the technology had "immense potentialities as regards human welfare."[8]

A type of nuclear bomb called the "Fat Man" is on view at the Los Alamos Scientific Laboratory Museum on October 15, 1965. Niels Bohr joined the team of scientists at Los Alamos, New Mexico, that built this type of atomic bomb that was dropped on Nagasaki, Japan, at the end of World War II.

So he agreed to help the Allies develop the weapon. He and his son joined the team of scientists in Los Alamos, New Mexico, that built the atom bomb that ended World War II. He spent the remaining years of his life working to develop peaceful uses for atomic energy.

After the war, he returned to Denmark. He worked in his institute until 1962, when he died of a heart attack at age seventy-seven. For both the Danish Jews and the international community, he was the right person at the right time.

4 From the City to the Sea: Ebba Lund

Most of the Danes who helped save the Jews were not famous like Niels Bohr. Most were ordinary citizens. Some were young college students. After Germany invaded Denmark, several university students gathered together to find ways to resist the German occupation.

Ebba Lund was a twenty-year-old chemical engineering student in 1943. She joined one of the student groups that were active in the resistance. Eventually, she and her younger sister became part of *Holger Danske*, the underground group responsible for hundreds of acts of sabotage against the Germans. Her membership in this group put her in contact with the fleeing Jews.

Lund's involvement with the Jews began with the declaration of martial law in late August: "The whole thing started when . . . we lost our government . . . and we capsized the navy, and the Germans took the Danish soldiers and put them into a camp, and all this was unexpected. It resulted in a reaction in the population."[1]

The underground gave Lund a very specific assignment: "In the end of September and beginning of October 1943, it became my job to become the 'export leader' of *Holger Danske*—you understand what I mean by that: We had to bring people to Sweden."[2]

Members of the Danish resistance disarm a German soldier in broad daylight sometime in 1943. Ebba Lund became a member of the largest Danish resistance group, Holger Danske, which led to her involvement in rescuing Danish Jews.

Instead of allowing the Nazis to *deport* the Jews to camps, the resistance would *export* them to safety. Lund lived in Copenhagen; so did the majority of Denmark's Jews. Copenhagen was on the coast, right on the Øresund, the sound separating Denmark from Sweden. Lund's task was to find a way to "export" to Sweden any Jews who wanted to go.

In her first mission, Lund was entrusted with just two people, a husband and wife. The man had money to pay for someone to ferry him across the Øresund. But neither he nor Lund knew anyone with a boat.

Getting Boats

Thinking through her list of friends and acquaintances, Lund remembered someone who worked for a company that sold supplies to shippers. He would know people who owned boats. She asked him for help, and within an hour or two she had a boat and a pilot. This smuggling operation was the first of many successes. Lund spent time on the docks and found people eager to help their fellow citizens:

I got on very good terms with quite a number of fishermen in the northern harbor of Copenhagen, and we really trusted each other in a funny way that worked right away. I had right away three to five fishermen's boats that were willing to sail for me and did so.[3]

49

But she encountered a problem:

> *It cost a lot of money. . . . [The fishermen] wanted the money because they assumed that if they were taken by the Germans, they would lose their boats, and if they didn't have the boat, they didn't have anything, and I accepted that point of view.*[4]

The fishermen's wages were not the only expense. Taking thousands of people across the water a few at a time could not be done in one night. The refugees had to be hidden until their turn came. While in hiding, they had to eat, and food cost money. Often they came to the coast in taxis, and the taxi drivers needed to be paid.

Collecting money actually turned out to be easy. Lund and her friends in Holger Danske simply asked people to contribute. Two of her classmates gathered a million *kroner* (the Danish currency) in just a few days. They went to the large, expensive houses of people their parents knew. One of the fund-raisers later realized, "It was probably naïve of us to drive around and entrust our secret undertakings to all those people. But in a strange way our naïveté was our strength. It disarmed people."[5]

The wealthy were not the only ones to give. Money came in from everywhere in amounts small and large. When ordinary people found out who was doing the work of transporting Jews to the harbors, they brought them money. Strangers approached rescuers on the streets and carefully slipped them bills and coins. In Bispebjerg Hospital, the head nurse kept a shoe box on her desk and people dropped in what they could for the rescue effort.

Danish fishermen used this boat, named "Sunshine," to transport Jews to Sweden. Ebba Lund found boats and pilots to help ferry Danish Jews to Sweden.

Danish resistance to German occupation was slow to form. The event that triggered widespread defiance was the attempt to deport the Jews.

> The Danes, being a peace-loving and easygoing people, had been reluctant for several years to take an active part in the resistance movement. But when the Germans started to persecute the Jews, when people had to hide relatives and friends, it meant that they were taking the first step in engaging in illegal activities against the Germans. This encouraged them to go even further and, as a consequence, the resistance movement grew enormously.[6]

The largest resistance group called itself *Holger Danske*. The name referred to a hero of legend. He was said to rise from his sleep to save Danes whenever they were in trouble. By the end of the war, it numbered more than three hundred people.

The Danish resistance was responsible for more than 4,700 acts of sabotage against factories, military buildings, ports, and railroads.[7] The groups were so successful at sabotaging trains that German soldiers stationed in Norway were delayed in reaching the battlefront in France. What should be a five-hour trip took ten days. When the Crown Princess gave birth to a baby, the resistance celebrated with its version of a twenty-one-gun salute: twenty-one simultaneous acts of sabotage.

Resisting the Nazis was dangerous. In all, 3,213 resistance fighters were killed.

Getting to the Boats

Once she had the boats and money, Lund's next problem was logistic: How would she get the people from their hiding places in the city to the boats on the shore? There were so

The largest resistance group in Denmark called itself Holger Danske, referring to a legendary Danish hero. This is a statue of the hero.

many people! Fortunately, Lund's mother and father lived near the coastline. She could keep refugees in their home. But how would she get them there? With others in the underground, she devised a plan.

The underground was a loosely organized assortment of several groups. Each group did what it could and connected with other groups. Most of the people in one group did not know people in the others. Members went by code names. Instead of a name, Lund had a hat. She was known as the girl in the red cap. She walked the streets of Copenhagen and let the refugees find her.

The Jews in Copenhagen hid in a number of different spots. The underground had established "collection points" where refugees gathered. Most of the hospitals were collection points. So was the Nordic Bookstore, directly across the street from Gestapo headquarters. The underground spread the word that anyone bound for Sweden should look for the girl in the red cap. When one or two found her, they went together to the coast, like friends enjoying an outing. After enough had gathered for a trip across the sound, getting to the boats was simple:

> From [my parents' home], together with my friends, I would essentially take taxis out to the harbor, but I never permitted the taxis to go into the harbor. We would have to walk, or go on bicycle, with the luggage on our backs as we went. Nothing else was permitted.[8]

Jewish refugees from the island of Falster, Denmark, travel aboard a fishing boat going to Sweden.

Some of the people involved in the rescue ferried their passengers at night. But Lund did not want to risk being caught out after curfew. Instead, her little groups went to the docks in broad daylight. She usually arranged for three or four boats at a time. This would be the typical size of a fishing fleet. The refugees looked like teams of fishermen, out for the day's catch. Each boat had a passenger cabin that could hold twenty-five or thirty-five people—if they squeezed in tightly.

Lund did not worry about the refugees being caught. The coast guard that patrolled the harbor was Danish, and its sailors did not stop the "export" vessels. The German patrol boats were in dry dock for "repairs," thanks to Duckwitz. German soldiers or Gestapo guarded the shore, but many of them did not want to arrest civilians.

None of the rescuers kept lists of the people they saved. They did not even know their names. The girl in the red cap could only estimate the number of people she helped. Her best guess was that she put between five hundred and eight hundred people on boats in October 1943. Every one of them made it to Sweden.[9]

After the Rescue

When the Jews were safely in Sweden, Lund returned to the original work of Holger Danske: sabotaging German interests. In February 1944, someone betrayed the group to the Germans. At that time, Lund was in a hospital, recovering from blood poisoning. She remained free when four members of the resistance group were arrested.

After the war, she resumed her studies and graduated with a specialty in microbiology. She became well known for research in veterinary science. She worked and taught in prestigious institutions in both Sweden and Denmark. Before her death in 1999, Ebba Lund spoke to a reporter about her part in the rescue. She was proud of the fact that everyone she helped was saved. "This," she said, "is the delight of my life."[10]

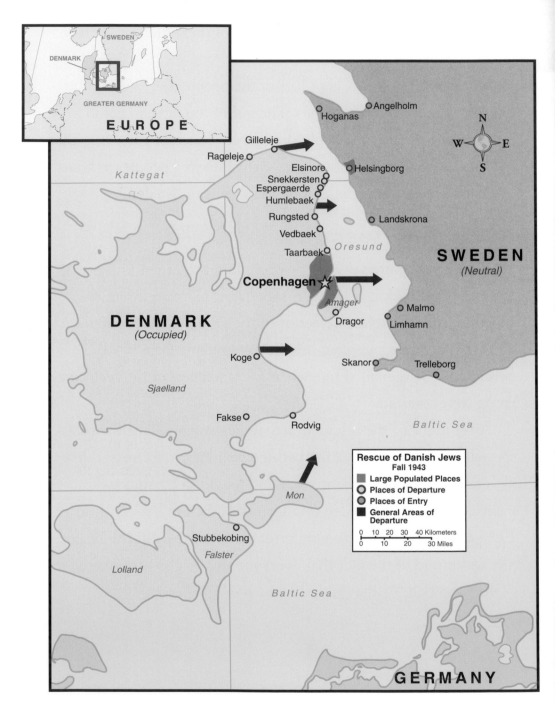

This map shows the many escape routes that were used to rescue the Danish Jews in October 1943, including points of departure in Denmark and points of entry in Sweden.

Some become heroes because they are the right people or they are in the right place. Erling Kiær was neither. He was a bookbinder living in the quiet coastal town of Elsinore, twenty-five miles from Denmark's capital.

Most of Denmark's Jews resided in Copenhagen. People in other towns were slow to learn about the Gestapo *Aktion*. But some Jews had come to Elsinore, where the distance to Sweden was very short. One of Kiær's friends suggested to Kiær that helping the Jews would be a way to anger the Germans. Kiær was not Jewish, but he hated what the Germans were doing in his country, so the idea appealed to him. He became a hero because he wanted to frustrate the Germans.

Forming a Plan

Kiær and his friend, Børge Rønne, did not stumble into being rescuers. They went about it deliberately. They recruited people they thought might be helpful. One was Danish police detective Thomod Larsen. They thought he would be able to learn useful information from the German police. Another was Dr. Jørgen Gersfelt. He had a home in the fishing village of Snekkersten, a short distance from Elsinore. It was an ideal place for hiding people until they could get them to a boat. And, of course, they recruited fishermen with boats.

In October 1943, several escape routes sprang up along the eastern coast of Denmark. The largest one was from Copenhagen, where Ebba Lund and others operated. Two to three thousand Jews crossed the sound along this route. Many were hidden on the northern edge of Copenhagen, in a town called Lyngby. Some Danes who were living in Sweden organized what became known as the Danish-Swedish Refugee Service. Their route was far south of the capital. The trip was much longer, but there were not as many patrols. More than seven hundred Jews reached safety through the Danish-Swedish Refugee Service. Kiær operated north of Copenhagen.

At Elsinore, the Øresund was very narrow; Sweden was only two and a half miles away. A number of fishing communities dotted the shore near Elsinore: Gilleleje, Snekkersten, Espergærde, and Humlebæk. This meant that refugees could board the boats from several different spots. Friendly people were willing to put strangers up in their cottages, inns, and churches. Daring adventurers volunteered to guide them from their hiding places to the waiting boats. The arrangement seemed perfect. Kiær and his friends gave their little group a code name: the Elsinore Sewing Club.

Gersfelt proved to be a very important member of the club. He knew people in Snekkersten, a beach resort for many Danes from Copenhagen. The doctor watched a number of homes for the owners, who used them only in the summer. In October, he had keys to several empty houses. As a doctor, Gersfelt had permission to be out after curfew. He also had larger rations of gas. He could drive refugees from the safe houses to the boats. He knew the area very well, including the back roads the Germans did not know. He generally drove the people who could not walk the short distance to the shore—the old and the young.

The young were a particular challenge for the group. The waters around Elsinore were patrolled by the Germans. That meant the rescuers had to appear to be fishing. They had to keep their illegal passengers hidden, often for hours. What would happen if a child cried out? How could they be sure little ones would not give everything away?

Dr. Gersfelt had an answer. He concocted a drug that put them to sleep. The potion worked so well that frightened mothers often worried that their infants would not wake up. However, of the hundreds of children injected, not one died of an overdose.

The Operation

The fishing boats at the northern edge of the Øresund were small. Most could take only a few refugees at a time, and they had to make many trips. One sixteen-year-old who worked on his father's boat described what a typical rescue was like:

> They went down [through the trapdoor] and disappeared in the hull. If they squeezed up, it could carry five or six. They could only take one little bag for the

journey. . . . Once they were all in the hold,
we shut the trapdoor, and we stacked our
ropes on top. The Germans who inspected
the boat never suspected that under the nets
and ropes there was a trapdoor! We made
many trips to Sweden. . . . [The crossing
would take] an hour and a half [to] two
hours, depending on sea conditions.[1]

Evacuating thousands of people five or six at a time was slow work. Kiær and his friends devised a second plan. Because the sound at Elsinore was so narrow, a ferry operated there. Railroad cars bringing iron ore and other materials from Sweden to Germany came across the Øresund on the ferry. After the ferry unloaded its cargo, the empty cars were sent back across the sound for more supplies. Why should the cars travel to Sweden empty when so many people were desperate to make the same trip?

Members of the underground snuck aboard the ferry just before it was to make its return trip to Sweden. The empty train cars had been inspected by the Germans, closed, and sealed shut. The daring rescuers broke the seals and filled the cars with escaping Jews. They sealed the cars again with seals they either stole or forged. They made sure the people inside could breathe. The scheme worked until a Swedish paper published a story about it, and the Nazis kept closer guard on the empty cars. Then the

Elsinore Sewing Club found the fishing boats were again the only means of escape.

Expanding the Operation

Kiær was frustrated with the slow pace of the rescue. So many people were still in danger. So few fishermen were able to help. He could not possibly get all the Jews across the sound at this rate. And the Germans were coming closer to uncovering their operation. What he needed was a bigger vessel that

There was a heavy German presence in Elsinore. But the Elsinore Sewing Club held secret meetings all over town, even at the German headquarters. This was the German consulate building in Elsinore.

could carry more people. He needed someone who could devote his full time to piloting it.

The need for a bigger boat was quickly met. One was sitting in the harbor at Elsinore, and no one was around it. Kiær "borrowed" it. The question of a pilot was also easily answered. Kiær would drive the boat himself. How hard could it be? To the surprise of his friends, the bookbinder became a boat captain overnight.

When the club received a large donation from a grateful Jew, Kiær returned the "borrowed" vessel and made a down payment on a large speedboat. Seventeen-year-old Preben Munch-Nielsen, one of the escorts who brought the refugees from their hideouts to the shore, described the importance of the larger boat:

> It was a . . . very good boat, a sound boat built in the beginning of the '30s. It was, of course, a wooden boat with a good engine and it was able to go rather quick, about eight or nine miles, and that is much for a motorboat. And when it started, Kiær . . . I remember, had two or three, no two trips to Sweden and I think we got ten to twelve passengers every time. And then later on we had in October seven hundred Jews and, totally I know that this boat brought about one thousand four hundred people from Denmark to Sweden.[2]

Preben Munch-Nielsen worked as an escort bringing Jewish refugees from their hideouts to the shore, where the boats transported them to Sweden.

If Munch-Nielsen's figures are accurate, Kiær had to cross the sound more than a hundred times. One of the greatest dangers to any boat making the crossing was the presence of German patrols. However, as Ebba Lund found farther south, not all the Germans were unkind. One Danish Jew, Ulrich Plesner, wrote of a surprising encounter with the enemy:

> On a dark and rough night, my neighbor sailed with lights out and the fish-hold full of Danish Jews. He was caught in the searchlight of a German Navy patrol boat which ordered him to stop and kept him covered. The German captain shouted: "What are you carrying?" And Ole [the neighbor] shouted back, "Fish." The captain then jumped onto the deck, leaving his crew to cover him, and demanded that the hatches to the fish-holds be removed.

> *He stared a long time at several dozen frightened people looking up at him. Finally, he turned and said to Ole, in a loud voice that could be heard by his own crew as well: "Ah, fish!" Then he returned to his boat and sailed into the night.*[3]

Caught

A less kind German captain put an end to Kiær's career as a pilot. After the Jews were safely in Sweden, the Elsinore Sewing Club continued to operate. Others needed to escape the Nazis also—saboteurs who had been identified and Allied soldiers who had been shot down over Denmark. Kiær was happy to take them across the Øresund. Returning from one such crossing, Kiær found himself surrounded by German patrol boats. He was immediately taken into custody and interrogated ruthlessly:

> *They started with the truncheons [clubs]. It hurt insanely; it was almost unbearable. But since it did not lead to any result for the Germans, they stopped after some time. . . . They looked a little at each other, then they sent me back to the basement. They said that now I could rest to the next day, now I knew what I could expect. . . . The second and the third day were the worst, but when they had passed, I did not feel anything any more.*[4]

Despite the torture, Kiær did not give up any information. He was sent to a series of prisons and, finally, to the Porta concentration camp in Germany. There, he worked in the slate mines with little food and brutal guards. Conditions were so harsh that, he said, "a Dane died every third day."[5]

But Kiær did not die there. Every time he felt like giving up, he thought of his wife and children. He had sent them to Sweden, where they were safe. Just before the war ended, the Swedish Red Cross brought Kiær and others out of Porta and back to Denmark.

In Denmark, Kiær was reunited with the other founders of the Elsinore Sewing Club. The police detective, Thomod Larsen, had been shot by a German soldier on the beach at Snekkersten

TRAGEDY IN GILLELEJE

The fishing village of Gilleleje is on the northern tip of the Danish island of Zealand. It was one of the spots from which Danish fishermen ferried Jews across the Øresund to Sweden.

On the night of October 6, 1943, about eighty Jews were waiting their turn to escape. The Elsinore Sewing Club had arranged for ships to meet them on the beach. But the Gestapo patrolled the area. The refugees needed to hide until the coast was clear. The underground took them all to a church in Gilleleje and told them to wait in the attic. They would set off an air raid alarm, making the Gestapo think British warplanes had been spotted. That would send the Germans indoors to seek cover. The false alarm would be the signal for the Jews to run for the boats.

But a Danish woman whose boyfriend was a German soldier had spotted the refugees. She became a *stikker*, the Danish word for an informer.

Before the air-raid signal could be sounded, German soldiers surrounded the church. They found the Jews hiding in the attic. They were among the nearly five hundred sent to the concentration camp at Theresienstadt. The only one who escaped was a young boy who climbed into the bell tower and hid among the church's bells.

A family of Jewish refugees sitting in their rowboat in Sweden after a successful crossing from Denmark.

and left for dead. However, the underground got him to a hospital and then to Sweden. Rønne and Gersfelt also had to take refuge across the Øresund. All came back to Denmark when the war was over. For many years afterward, they met once a month at a coffee shop in Elsinore. They talked of old times and rejoiced in the freedom they enjoyed—a freedom they helped maintain.

6 Saved! Leo Goldberger

Like most other Danes, Denmark's Jews were little affected by German occupation for the first two and a half years. For Leo Goldberger, life went on as it always had. His father was one of two chief cantors in Copenhagen's largest synagogue. His job was to sing during the religious services. The family was loved and respected in the community. The second oldest of four children, Leo was as happy and carefree as any thirteen-year-old.

But on August 28, 1943, young Goldberger's happy innocence came to an end. That was the day before the Danish government dissolved. The German authority in Denmark, Werner Best, had given the Danes a list of demands. To put pressure on them, Best arrested a number of Danes. He would let the hostages go when the government met the demands. But the government did not cooperate. So on the next day, Germany declared a state of emergency and the Danish government resigned. One of the people arrested was the chief rabbi of the synagogue. Another on the list of more than a dozen officials and prominent Jews was Leo Goldberger's father, Eugene.

As they often did, the Germans made their move when the city slept. The teenager described the attempted arrest:

Leo Goldberger (left) and his older brother, Milan, appear in this photo taken in 1934.

> *My father quickly came into my brother's and my room and whispered that the Germans were outside and that he would not under any circumstances open the door. For me, this was the most terror-filled moment I had ever experienced. The insistent loud knocks of rifle butts. Fearing that they would break down the door any minute, I implored my father to open it, but he was determined not to. Then in the nick of time, we heard our upstairs neighbor's voice telling the German soldiers that we—the Goldbergers—were away for the summer, and that three o'clock in the morning was in any case no time to make such a racket.[1]*

The neighbor's quick thinking had saved them. But the Gestapo did not leave. The police waited outside the apartment building. After spending the night in their cellar's bomb shelter, Goldberger and his two oldest sons joined the remaining family members in their rented summerhouse near Helsingør.

Two or three weeks later, the country seemed to return to normal. Except for the fact that the military was in control rather than civilian officers, Denmark appeared much the same as it had for the past two years. Leo's father thought it was safe to return to Copenhagen. As a cantor, he needed to be at the synagogue for the Rosh Hashanah celebration about two weeks away.

Eluding Capture

When Leo's father, Eugene, heard the rabbi's announcement of the coming German *Aktion*, he knew he must leave immediately. He was already a wanted man. No place in Denmark would be safe for him or his family.

On the night of the raid, the Goldbergers were not in Copenhagen. They were hiding with a wealthy family thirty-five miles away. But their hosts were also Jewish. They, too, were in danger, and the house would not be safe for long. The hosts had already thought about escaping to Sweden. They asked Eugene if he wanted to go in with them to pay someone to take them across the sound.

The first days of the rescue were very chaotic. People who could afford to hire fishermen did so without any help. The boatmen, unaware of the great danger and the greater numbers to come later, generally charged the refugees what seemed reasonable to them—one thousand to ten

Eugene Goldberger, Leo's father, is pictured wearing the traditional attire of a cantor. When Germany seized control of the Danish government, Eugene Goldberger was placed on an arrest list of prominent Jews.

Paying for the passage of Jews escaping from Denmark was a problem. Once in Sweden, refugees still needed money until they could get jobs. This is the inside of an invitation to a gala concert in New York City on February 17, 1944, to benefit the Danish refugees.

thousand *kroner* ($200–$2000) per person. As the number of refugees swelled and people understood the situation, many fishermen dropped their fee to five hundred *kroner*. Many others charged nothing. The resistance raised funds for the large number who could not afford to pay.

The Goldbergers, however, were among the first to reach the coast. No rescue operations were yet organized. They did not have enough money for passage for six people. It would cost more than Eugene made in an entire year. They slept uneasily that first night, with no idea what they would do.

When they awoke, they found their hosts gone. Their hosts could afford the fee the boatman asked, and they left everything behind and went to Sweden. They had not even said good-bye.

Eugene Goldberger was sick with fear. He had heard stories of how the Nazis treated Jews in other countries. Taking a train back to Copenhagen, he tried to make a plan. Who did he know that might have contact with a friendly fisherman? Was there anyone he might ask to lend him the money? Could he get an advance on his salary?

To Safety

His thoughts were interrupted by a woman's concerned voice. The fellow passenger was not a Jew, but she recognized him. She noticed Goldberger's worried expression and asked what was troubling him. He told her the whole story. To his surprise, the woman—practically a complete stranger—offered to help. They arranged to meet a few hours later.

The financial help did not come from the woman. She simply made the connections. The money—about 25,000 *kroner*—came from a Christian pastor. Like the woman, he was a stranger to Goldberger. But he wanted Goldberger to escape.

The next night, the six Goldbergers stood on a beach with about twenty other refugees. They shivered in the cold as they waited for a boat to flash its lights. Leo described what happened when the signal finally came:

> *My youngest brother, barely three years old, had been given a sleeping pill to keep him quiet. . . . Wading straight into the sea, we walked out some 100 feet through icy water, in water that reached up to my chest. My father carried my two small brothers on his arm. . . . I clutched my precious flashlight. My older brother tried valiantly to carry the suitcases but finally had to let them drop in the water. We were hauled aboard the boat, directed in whispers to lie concealed in the cargo area, there to stretch out covered by smelly canvases; in the event German patrols were to inspect the boat, we would be passed over as fish. . . . As we proceeded out toward the open sea, my father chanted a muted prayer.[2]*

Hundreds of other families left their native Denmark in similar fashion. Leif Donde, very young at the time, remembered the cold, the flight, and the hiding:

> *We were told that . . . we couldn't bring any luggage whatsoever. That we should put on as many warm clothes as we possibly could, and we went over and stayed overnight with . . . some friends of my parents. . . . [T]his happened time and again during*

the escape to Sweden, that we were told, "Try not to be conspicuous." That's very, very important. . . . I understood that this was serious, but I did also feel that to some extent this was an adventure. I don't think you can expect much else from a six-year-old kid.[3]

Children may have seen the escape as an adventure, but adults knew the peril. With every passing day, the danger of discovery and capture increased. German patrol boats began stopping the vessels. Some even looked under the fish-smelling canvases. On some shores, the Gestapo used dogs to sniff for hidden people.

The refugees worried the entire time they were in Danish waters.

Safe at Last

The Goldbergers' journey took hours. They traveled at night, so they were never sure what was over the next wave.

Leif Donde, pictured here in Copenhagen, was six years old when he made the flight from Denmark to Sweden.

KING CHRISTIAN X: MYTH AND REALITY

Christian X was king of Denmark through two world wars. Stories about the king arose during the German occupation. One story says that when Germany wanted to make a law that all Jews in Denmark must wear the Star of David, the king said he would wear it also. Another story says that the law was passed and the king actually wore the emblem on his arm. A third story has all the people of Denmark wearing the armband. None of the stories is true. They persist because Leon Uris repeated them in his popular book, *Exodus*, published in 1958.

King Christian on one of his famous rides through the streets of Copenhagen in 1940. He rode his horse through the streets to connect with his people.

The truth is that King Christian always regarded the Jews as citizens no different from any other Danes. He told this to the Germans. Germany never required the Jewish badge in Denmark.

The king had a regular habit of riding his horse through the city every morning. It was his way of connecting with his people. During the occupation, he continued with his custom, instilling pride in his citizens. He let them know that Denmark was not completely under Germany's rule.

The myths have persisted because Christian was a popular king. Even those who disapproved of his cooperation with Germany loved him. His defiant morning ride became a symbol of Danish resistance. To signify their patriotism and their resistance to German occupation, many Danes wore a king's emblem pin. It had a crown and the king's insignia: a C with an X inside, for Christian X (the tenth).

Leo Goldberger lived in Sweden with his family until Denmark was liberated in 1945. Some children escaped Denmark without their parents; Sweden had places of refuge for them, too. This group of Jewish children lived in a children's home in Sweden after their escape from Denmark.

They remained below deck, in the cargo hold, fearing the sudden appearance of a German vessel. After what must have seemed like an eternity, the fishermen spotted lights in the distance. They dotted the shore, the shore of Sweden! Finally, all six were safe.

The family stayed in Sweden until the war ended. Eugene found a job as a cantor in a small Swedish synagogue in the city of Gøteborg.

When Denmark was liberated in 1945, the Goldbergers returned to their home in Copenhagen. It had been empty for more than a year and a half. Yet no one had bothered it; nothing was missing. The Goldbergers' neighbors were happy to have them back. Throughout the country, the same scene occurred in house after house. The Danes had cared for the property of their Jewish friends while they were away. They had watered plants and fed pets. They were, after all, neighbors.

Leo Goldberger later emigrated to the United States. He became a professor of psychology at New York University. Goldberger remains grateful to the Danish people, who he calls "truly fantastic."[4]

Not all of Denmark's Jews were rescued on the night of the Rosh Hashanah raid. The Krasnik family was among the unfortunate ones. Neither Isaac, nor his wife, Rachel, nor their five-year-old daughter, Birgit, heard the rabbi's announcement. Instead of being in the synagogue that fateful morning, they were in a German police station.

The Krasniks were not criminals. They owned a tailor shop in Copenhagen. They had friends in the community. They were happy and, even after the German army entered, they felt safe. But, Birgit wrote:

> Life was marked by a certain anxiety. We heard many rumors about the assault on the Jews in Germany and Poland. But we chose to push these ghastly things from our minds. They were so far away from peaceful Denmark.[1]

When the Germans declared martial law, however, Denmark did not seem so peaceful or safe. Birgit's parents had decided to leave. Her father had the name of a fisherman who had taken some Jews across the sound to Sweden. He went to the docks to arrange for passage for himself and his family. This was dangerous because Germany had forbidden all travel to Sweden. A Danish informer heard the conversation and reported it to the Gestapo. Krasnik was arrested.

Deceived

When her husband did not return home, Rachel went to Gestapo headquarters. She was told that Isaac was in custody, but he would be brought to the station the next day. She must come back with her daughter Birgit. Isaac would be released and they could take him home.

Years later, Birgit wondered why her mother did not suspect a trick. Why would a five-year-old need to come to the station? How did the Gestapo even know her name? Rachel did not think of such questions. When she and Birgit went to the station the next day, they were escorted into a dark room filled with people— all of them Jews. All were there to meet relatives who were to be released from custody. All had been told to bring their entire family. A sense of dread settled on the waiting captives, including Birgit, who later wrote:

> The entire atmosphere in the place was marked by uncertainty. . . . Could there be something in the rumor that had circulated about a pending deportation of Denmark's Jewish population? My mother was completely white in the face and she gave me explicit instructions to be silent. . . . She had discovered that we had gone straight into the lion's den.[2]

Transported

While Birgit and her mother were at Gestapo headquarters, her grandparents were preparing a festive table. The New Year's celebration would begin that night. They decorated, prepared special food, and gathered all of Birgit's aunts and uncles. When a knock sounded, they expected Birgit and her parents to join them, so they opened the door eagerly. Instead of family, two stone-faced German soldiers stood in the opening.

At about the same time, soldiers also appeared at Gestapo headquarters. With guns drawn, they drove all the Jews out into the street. Birgit was herded along with everyone else into waiting trucks. Bars on the windows made it difficult to see where the trucks were headed. When they finally stopped, the prisoners found themselves at the waterfront.

The captives were lined up along the dock. They were told to face the sea and stand completely still. This was not easy for a frightened five-year-old. Birgit was not dressed for the October night. She shivered and tried to keep from crying. The cold silence was broken with a new order:

> We should get on board the big gray ship.
> . . . I had never been on board such a large
> ship before; it was a frightening experience.
> We were taken below deck—all the way down
> at the bottom. There were a lot of weird
> smells and the air was dense and clammy.
> There was nothing to sit on.[3]

Eventually, the little girl sank to the floor and closed her eyes. The drone of the ship's engines lulled her to sleep. When she awoke, she found that more people had been brought on board. Her father was there, as were her other relatives. The ship, *Wartheland*, had been prepared to carry five thousand Jews out of Denmark. It left the harbor with only 202.[4]

When the ship docked in Germany, the journey was not over:

It was a brutal encounter with a world far from my safe upbringing in the apartment home in Copenhagen. None of us had anything to eat. . . . Not far from the harbor was a train with many cars. Not a passenger train with benches to sit on. No it was a cattle train. Several of the adults began to protest against going into the cars. . . . It was pointless to protest. The German soldiers threatened to loose the dogs on us.[5]

The train was even more unbearable than the gray ship. The captives spent hours with no food, no rest, no toilets, and no privacy. The horrible ordeal ended at the Theresienstadt concentration camp.

Theresienstadt

All the new arrivals stood in lines as they were counted and recounted. Then came the stripping. Everything they had became

THERESIENSTADT

The town of Theresienstadt (also called Terezín) was built as a military outpost. It was established in 1784 by Austrian Emperor Josef II and named after his mother, Theresa. In November 1941, Hitler turned it into a concentration camp.

Theresienstadt is sometimes called a ghetto because it looked like a town. It is sometimes called a camp because it was operated like the other camps. It was essentially a brutal prison. The primary purpose of Theresienstadt was to deceive people. It was a propaganda tool.

Hitler called Theresienstadt a "model camp." He used it to show the world that Germany treated the Jews well. Originally, three types of German and Austrian Jews were kept there: the elderly; wounded or decorated World War I veterans; and well-known prisoners, especially artists and musicians. Others were sent to what Hitler called "labor camps." The Nazis would have a hard time explaining why elderly and disabled Jews were made to work; sending them to a "retirement town" made sense.

Theresienstadt was far from a model place. Conditions were as deplorable as in the other camps. Guards were as brutal. The camp became a transit camp—a place for prisoners to stay briefly before being shipped "to the east"—to other labor camps and to the death camps. In its three and a half years of existence, 140,000 Jews spent some time in Theresienstadt. Of these, 90,000 were deported east (where most died) and 33,000 perished in the camp.

Otto Samisch, a prisoner at Theresienstadt, painted this watercolor landscape of the camp in 1943. Despite the terrible living conditions, the camp had a developed cultural life.

When the Red Cross representatives inspected the camp, they did not know that, to make the "town" appear less crowded, 7,500 people had just been deported to the death camp of Auschwitz.

the property of their captors. The one thing Birgit treasured was taken from her—a small bracelet with a shiny heart. It was a child's toy, of no military or economic worth. But she could not keep anything.

The prisoners in Theresienstadt did not have to give up their clothes. They did, however, have to sew a patch on the clothing. It was a yellow Star of David with the word *Jude* ("Jew") emblazoned across it. For centuries, the six-pointed star had been the proud symbol of the Jewish people. For Birgit, the badge told her that others saw her as different.

Upon arrival at Theresienstadt, all camp inmates had to sew a Star of David patch on their clothes.

The camp guards noticed that Birgit's mother was pregnant. The Nazis did not want women to have babies in the camp, so they told her they would perform an abortion. Rachel was horrified. Thinking quickly, she lied about how far along she was in her pregnancy. The camp "doctors" performed abortions only in the early stages of pregnancy, so she said she was in a later stage. The guards believed her. Four months later, Birgit's brother Preben was born.

Theresienstadt was a little better than many of the German concentration camps because the Nazis used it as a showplace to

Female prisoners sleep on the floor of barracks in the women's camp in Theresienstadt. Crowded and filthy conditions in the camp allowed disease to spread easily.

try to convince outsiders that their camps were decent facilities. Still, Theresienstadt was a horrible place. It was terribly crowded; most people slept at least two or three in a bed. The mattresses were made of straw and covered with thin, dirty blankets. Fleas and lice spread deadly diseases. Food rations were miserably small.

The worst part was the constant fear. People disappeared regularly as transports came to "resettle" them to the east. In their attempt to rid Europe of all its Jews, the Nazis regularly sent groups from the camp to death camps in Poland. Even at age five, Birgit was frightened at the thought of going away: "There were many rumors of transports in the camp, and I was terrified of the transports. I did not know where they went, but I knew they never came back."[6]

Life-Saving Packages

The people in Denmark did not forget the Jews in Theresienstadt. Denmark's government asked to visit the camp and send packages to the Danes there. For weeks Germany refused. But the Danes did not give up. Years earlier, Germany, along with many other nations, had signed the Geneva Convention. According to this agreement, Germany was supposed to allow the Red Cross to visit prisoners of war. So the Danish government kept pressing the issue. Still refusing any visit, Germany said the Red Cross could deliver letters and clothing to the Danish prisoners.

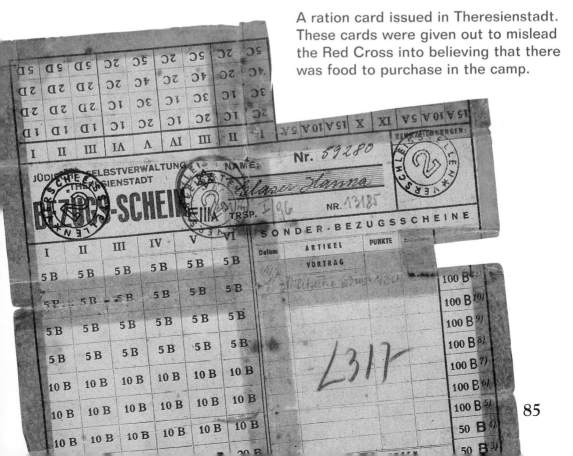

A ration card issued in Theresienstadt. These cards were given out to mislead the Red Cross into believing that there was food to purchase in the camp.

As with the rescue by sea, private citizens rose to the opportunity. One was Richard Ege, a professor at the Rockefeller Institute of Biochemistry in Copenhagen. In the first weeks of October, his home and the Institute had been collection points for Jews. He and his wife had donated and collected money for the rescue. Now they organized volunteers to gather clothing.

When the Nazis would not allow the Danes to send food or medicine in their Red Cross parcels, Ege contacted drug companies. He had them make a special pill for the parcels—a strong multivitamin. Ege oversaw a group of thirty-five people who worked full-time sending the packages. Birgit's newborn brother was kept alive by the powdered milk in the parcels from home.

Red Cross Visit

Still, the leaders in Denmark did not rest. They wanted someone to visit Theresienstadt and see the condition of their people. Finally, Germany gave in to the unrelenting pressure from Denmark. The Red Cross would be allowed to inspect the camp in June 1944. In the weeks before the visit, the camp was busy. One prisoner recalled:

> When the Red Cross came in July (sic) 1944, the Nazis put up dummy stores, a cafe, kindergarten and flower gardens to give the impression that we were leading "normal" lives. We painted the house fronts on the inspection routes and the Nazis gave us extra food—one extra dumpling each.[7]

The people at the camp put on quite a show. They organized a soccer game and presented a children's opera in the newly built concert hall. They appointed one of the Jews mayor for the day and chauffeured him around the "town." They hoped the inspectors would ignore the bruise under the "mayor's" eye.

Birgit spent the day of the inspection playing in the new playground. The Germans wanted the delegates to see happy children. Birgit was indeed happy. She had not had such toys since her arrival at the camp. She would not have them the next day either. After the guests left, all the playthings were taken away. Bars were placed around the playground. Life returned to what had become "normal."

This scene staged by the Nazis for the Red Cross inspection in June 1944 shows children playing in a park.

The show appeared to work; the Red Cross report on Theresienstadt was good. Later, one delegate said the inspectors were not completely fooled, but they did not want to upset the Germans. They were afraid the Germans might not permit the prisoners to receive their care packages. And, unlike the visit, the packages saved lives.

Home

Almost a year after the first Red Cross visit, Birgit again saw the white flag with its Red Cross. It was on buses—lots of buses. The Swedish Red Cross had made an arrangement with the Nazis to take all of the Danes in Theresienstadt to Sweden. The date was April 15, 1945. Fifteen days later, Hitler committed suicide. Seven days after that, Germany surrendered, and the war ended. But on April 15, Birgit's long nightmare was ending. With her father, her mother, and her baby brother, she climbed into one of the white buses. The Swedish buses took 423 Danish Jews out of the camp. Only fifty-one had died.

In her adult years, Birgit married and made a life for herself in Denmark. She is chairwoman of the Theresienstadt Society, an organization of former prisoners of the camp. She travels and speaks to schoolchildren about her experience and the rescue of the Danish Jews.

8 Sweden Helps: Count Folke Bernadotte

The rescue of the Danish Jews would not have been possible without the help of Sweden. The government and people of Sweden gave them refuge. Swedish sailors brought them safely to shore. One of those who escaped across the Øresund, Tove Bamberger, recalled her relief at seeing Swedish boats:

> When we were in the middle of the ocean . . . between Sweden and Denmark, a big boat came and we were afraid it was Germans because there were soldiers on it. They were dressed . . . just like Germans. But it was a Swedish patrol boat that came to pick us up. They came in Swedish waters. . . . Then we were safe—the Germans couldn't do anything. There came the big boat and they helped us up from the fishing boat. And we stayed on the deck. Then we were, we were saved.[1]

For at least a year and a half, the Jewish refugees remained safe because of the kindness and generosity of Swedish citizens. Bamberger remembered: "They're welcoming us. . . . [They gave us] coffee, tea, and they told us where we could stay. They put us actually in the Grand Hotel. . . . They paid for the suites, paid for everything, and they said we could stay there."[2]

One Swede played a major role in rescuing the Danish Jews in Theresienstadt: Count Folke Bernadotte.

A Swedish Gentleman

Bernadotte was a nobleman, the grandson of a former king. He had been an officer in the Swedish cavalry and had represented Sweden at international events in the United States. He was a gentleman, an officer, and a diplomat.

A Swedish policeman accompanies a Jewish refugee to the welfare office in Rebslagergade, Sweden. The rescue of the Danish Jews would not have been possible without help from the people of Sweden.

In 1859, Swiss businessman Henry Dunant happened to witness a battle while on a trip in Italy. He was appalled at the terrible suffering of the wounded. He tended to the wounded soldiers and convinced others to help them. When he returned to his home in Geneva, he organized a series of international conferences to get people to agree to treat soldiers wounded in battle humanely.

Out of these conferences, the Geneva Conventions were born. A convention is a formal agreement. The Geneva Conventions are four treaties signed in Geneva, Switzerland, that set standards for international law.

The conferences also gave birth to the Red Cross/Red Crescent movement in 1863. Red Cross/Red Crescent organizations help wounded soldiers, prisoners of war, and civilians affected by war and other disasters. They are completely neutral, not taking sides in any conflict. They give humanitarian aid, regardless of nationality, race, religion, economics, or politics.

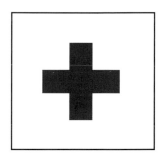

The Red Cross/Red Crescent is an international movement, but each country has its own organization. Each official organization is part of the International Federation of Red Cross and Red Crescent Societies. The American Red Cross was established in 1881.

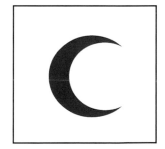

The symbol of a red cross on a white background was selected as a reverse image of the flag of Switzerland, a country that has been neutral in every war. The Ottoman Empire (now Turkey) adopted a red crescent as its symbol as a reverse image of the flag of the empire. Neither symbol was meant to be religious, but they appear to have religious meaning for some. Therefore, the International Federation accepted a third symbol in 2005: the Red Crystal. A country can use whichever symbol it chooses, but every nation that has signed the Geneva Convention must respect all three.

Count Folke Bernadotte

He was also an organizer. Before World War II began, Bernadotte was director of the Swedish Boy Scouts. Seeing the dark clouds of war coming, he prepared his scouts to defend their country. He trained them to fight against tanks in case German troops invaded Sweden. He taught them first aid and basic medicine so they would be prepared to treat any wounded.

In 1945, he was vice president of the Swedish Red Cross. The mission of the Red Cross was to care for civilians suffering because of war. Some Western governments had tried to persuade Germany to release the civilians Germany had imprisoned in its concentration camps, but Germany would not negotiate with the governments. But the Red Cross was not a government agency. It was not political; it could not take sides in the war. German officials could talk freely with Red Cross representatives.

Denmark and Norway had not stopped trying to get their citizens freed from German camps. But they had not been successful. A Norwegian diplomat asked Sweden's Red Cross for help. He asked Sweden to try to talk Germany into releasing

Danish and Norwegian prisoners. The chairman of the Red Cross selected Bernadotte for the job.

Negotiator

Bernadotte's first reaction was hesitation. He wrote:

> Would it be possible for Sweden to do something to lessen the suffering caused by the German system of concentration camps—to save at least some of the unfortunates otherwise doomed to die in horrible conditions? I felt little optimism, for I was well aware that the German authorities had firmly rejected all suggestions, whether they came from the international or national Red Cross organizations, neutrals included. . . . The Germans absolutely declined to allow any foreigner a glimpse into these hells, as we feared them to be.[3]

Bernadotte may not have known that some Germans wanted to talk. Those Germans knew they were losing the war. They wanted to make deals. Bernadotte needed someone to connect him with those Germans. He found that person in Felix Kersten.

Kersten was a personal assistant to Heinrich Himmler, who was second in command to Hitler. Kersten lived in Sweden and went to Berlin when Himmler asked for him. Most of the Allies did not trust him, but he could get people in to see Himmler.

He had helped arrange a secret agreement that freed a hundred Norwegian students and Danish policemen. Perhaps he could introduce Bernadotte to this influential German. Bernadotte was not sure:

> *I had no illusions as to the difficulties of my task, and little hope of obtaining more than a partial success. Though well aware of the many obstacles in my path, I nevertheless persuaded myself that if I could only meet Himmler I could not fail to obtain some concession.*[4]

Bernadotte did meet with Himmler and several other Germans in high places. After two months of negotiating, Bernadotte got even more than he asked for. The Red Cross was able to evacuate more than 15,000 prisoners from German camps to Sweden, many of them Jews. Only about half were Scandinavian; the rest were from many different countries.

Rescuer

The Danes at Theresienstadt were among the last to be liberated. By April 1945, Allied armies were already in Germany. The Nazis were desperately trying to empty the camps and remove all evidence of their existence. They were murdering the prisoners and sending them on death marches deeper into Germany so they could destroy the camps. Bernadotte was in a race against time.

On April 12, he finally received permission to take the Danes from Theresienstadt. He immediately headed for the camp with twenty-three Red Cross buses, twelve private cars, several motor bikes, and a number of Danish ambulances.

The trip to the camp was dangerous. It wound through areas where German and Soviet armies were shooting at each other. Trucks carrying German soldiers were all along the roads. The Allies were flying over the supply routes, dropping bombs on troop convoys. From the air, the large Red Cross vehicles could easily be confused with troop transports. To distinguish the buses from the drab green military trucks, Bernadotte painted them white. To further identify them as non-combatant, he painted huge red crosses on the sides.

Himmler had not made the rescue easy for Bernadotte. He had forbidden the Swedes to take or purchase anything in Germany. They had to bring everything with them. So the Red Cross procession included hospital buses, a field kitchen, and trucks that held food, gasoline, and other supplies and equipment.

Himmler had also required that Gestapo agents ride on the buses. After all, the rescued people were prisoners of Germany. So until they reached neutral Sweden, the 423 Danes from Theresienstadt held their breath. The two-day journey through northern Germany was somber. When the Gestapo raised the shades on the buses' windows, the Danes were stunned by the wreckage they saw. The once lovely German countryside was pocked with craters from Allied bombs. Beautiful cities lay in ruins.

A group of Polish female prisoners listen to an address from Bernadotte at the Ravensbrück camp in Germany. They are all marked with a white X indicating their selection for evacuation under the agreement Bernadotte made with Heinrich Himmler.

But when they crossed into Denmark, the mood changed abruptly. Throngs of Danes lined the streets, cheering and waving wildly. "Welcome to Denmark!" they shouted. They pressed against the buses, reaching through the windows with flowers, candy, and other gifts. Bernadotte had not arranged this greeting. Just as the Danish people had risen spontaneously to save their neighbors, they came together spontaneously to receive them back.

The happy scene was repeated in many cities in Denmark. But the passengers were not free yet. Denmark remained an occupied country, and the Jews from Theresienstadt were still prisoners of the Gestapo. The German police drew their pistols and forced the crowds back. They threatened to return their charges to the camp in Germany. The people let the buses pass. They stood obediently silent, but their broad smiles and enthusiastic waves were wonderfully refreshing.

Even when they reached Copenhagen, home to many on the buses, they were not free. Himmler's arrangement with Bernadotte was for the prisoners to be taken to Sweden. At Copenhagen, they whispered good-bye to Denmark again and boarded a ferry. The Gestapo did not leave them until they had safely disembarked at Malmö, Sweden.

Within two months, the war was over and the Danes came home. Many had been gone for almost two years. Their homecoming was an occasion of great joy and surprise. The rabbi, who first warned them to leave, described the common reaction:

When we returned, our fellow Danes did say "welcome back." And how they said it—emotionally, with open arms and hearts. Our homes, our businesses, our property and money had been taken care of and returned to us. In most cases we found our homes newly painted, and there were flowers on the table. You cannot imagine how happy it made us feel to be back home. The welcome we received from the King, from everybody, is the most important event in Danish-Jewish history.[5]

Peacemaker

Bernadotte had proven himself trustworthy to Himmler. He had carried out his mission exactly as the two agreed. He had not caused Himmler any trouble or embarrassment. Consequently, when Himmler had a different kind of mission in mind, he sought out the Swedish count. The white buses were still rolling when Himmler and Bernadotte met secretly.

Himmler knew that the war was lost. But he also knew that Hitler was pushing his forces to fight harder. Himmler offered to surrender Germany's troops without Hitler's approval. He asked Bernadotte to take that message to the U.S. command. But there was a catch. Germany had been fighting on two fronts—Britain, the United States, and other Allies in the west, and the Soviet

Union in the east. Himmler wanted to surrender to the Western allies, but not to the Soviets.

Doubtful that the offer would be received, Bernadotte still delivered the message. At this time, the Allies were bombing Hitler's headquarters in Berlin. Much of Europe had already been liberated. The German army was in retreat and its defeat was only a matter of time. The Allies were willing to wait rather than give in to any conditions. They rejected Himmler's offer. Two weeks later, Germany surrendered unconditionally.

Bernadotte's skill at negotiation and peacemaking was recognized by many people. In 1948, when the newly formed nation of Israel was at war with its Arab neighbors, the United Nations (UN) asked Bernadotte to

Count Folke Bernadotte (center, hands on hips) walking with United Nations officials. After the war, he served as a mediator for the UN.

help stop the fighting. He was the first mediator, or go-between, in United Nations history. He tried to negotiate peace between the Israelis and the Arabs. But neither side would agree on a way to solve their differences. Members of an Israeli extremist group, angry at Bernadotte's suggestions for peace, shot and killed him. The man who rescued thousands of Jews was assassinated by Jews who wanted war instead of peace.

9 From Rescuer to Rescued: Jørgen Kieler

Many of the Danish rescuers became heroes because of circumstances. They were good people in the right places. Jørgen Kieler became a hero because of conscience.

Kieler, a non-Jew, had been to Germany. He had seen how brutal Hitler's Germany was. He was twenty-one when Germany invaded Denmark—old enough to resent the occupying force and young enough to actively resist it. "At the beginning of the German occupation," he recalled, "people were confused and in despair. We all thought that the Germans were going to win the war and we were asking ourselves what can we do?"[1]

Kieler had to do something. To not act was to allow the Germans to win. Kieler felt strongly that what the Nazis were doing in Germany and in Denmark was wrong. As a matter of conscience, he had to fight against them.

His first act of defiance was actually against his own government. He hated Denmark's cooperation with the occupiers. In November 1941, Germany pressured Denmark to sign the Anti-Comintern Pact. This action made Denmark an ally of Germany in its war against the Soviet Union. Most Danes did not want to be an ally of Germany in anything. Kieler, a medical student, joined many others in a public protest. Hundreds packed

A large crowd of students wearing white caps gathers in the Copenhagen Town Hall Square to protest the Anti-Comintern Pact on November 25, 1941.

the streets of Copenhagen, singing Danish anthems and loudly criticizing the government's actions. After several days, Germany demanded that the Danish police stop the demonstration. Kieler was one of several young people beaten up by the police.

Nonviolent Resistance

A few months later, Kieler took another step deeper into resistance. He helped print and distribute the underground newspaper *Frit Danmark* (*Free Denmark*). One of the few changes the Germans

Frit Danmark

2. Aarg. Nr. 5 — Udgivet af en Kreds af Danske — August 1943

Begivenhederne nærmer sig Danmark
Nu maa Rigsdagen handle

Saafremt den danske Rigsdag vil røgte det Hverv, Folket for blot nogle Maaneder siden tillidsfuldt lagde i dens Hænder, saa maa den nu, *netop nu*, offentligt, *netop offentligt*, give tilkende, at den efter de sidste Dages militære og storpolitiske Begivenheder er sig sit Ansvar bevidst.

Hvad Churchill, Roosevelt og Eisenhower har sagt til Italienerne, gælder for os som for alle af tysk Nazisme voldførte Folk: *de maa stege i deres eget Fedt*, og de maa lide Savn, Nød og Ydmygelse, og de maa finde sig i de Allieredes Land-, Sø- og Luftvaabens Hærgen, indtil de selv siger sig fri af direkte og indirekte Samarbejde med Hitler og hans korrupte Bander. Vover den danske Rigsdag at sidde disse Advarsler overhørig?

Uligheden mellem de Tilstande, som hersker i Danmark og i de egentlig krigsførende Lande, hvad enten de som Rumænien, Ungarn, Italien og Finland er Hitlers Forbundsfæller, eller de — som Frankrig — lever under en Slags Vaabenstilstands Kaar, eller de endelig er hans midlertidigt slagne Fjender som Norge, Belgien, Holland, Jugoslavien og Grækenland — — disse Uligheder er saa iøjnefaldende, at den ved ubehagelige Sammenligninger sædvanlig anvendte Replik: »Det er noget helt andet«, denne Gang ikke kan faa Betydning for andre end Analfabeter.

Det Spørgsmaal, som foreligger, skal ikke besvares ved Paavisning af Uligheder mellem Danmarks og f. Eks. Italiens Forhold til Hitler-Tyskland, men ved *Erkendelse af de Ligheder*, som efter de allierede Stormagters paa givne Kendsgerninger støttede Opfattelse vitterlig findes mellem Danmark og andre Lande, der tjener den tyske Krigsmaskine og derved unyttigt forlænger Krigen og selv paatager sig den dermed forbundne, uhyre Risiko.

Eller er det ikke en for Verden aabenbar Kendsgerning, at Danmark territorialt, økonomisk og finansielt lader sig udnytte af Hitler-Tyskland i Krigen mod de allierede Nationer?

Jo, det *er* en for Verden aabenbar Kendsgerning, at saadan, *netop saadan* spiller Danmark sin Rolle i Tidens Drama — og har spillet den uafbrudt siden 9. April 1940.

Vist saa, vil Indvendingerne lyde, vist saa, men under Protest og under Overmagts Tvang.

Lad gaa med Protesten. Den foreligger — vil vi da haabe — forsvarligt dokumenteret.

Men *Tvangen?* Lader ogsaa den sig dokumentere, vel at mærke saaledes, at dens Anvendelse ikke blot overbeviser os selv, men — hvad der i den givne Situation er afgørende — de allierede Stormagter?

Det er ikke tilstrækkeligt at fortælle om Trusler. Naturligvis har Tyskerne ruttet med Trusler. Truslen er den fejges Hovedvaaben. Spørgsmaalet er dette, *netop dette*, om den Scavenianske Regering har bøjet sig allerede for Truslerne, eller om den i store og smaa Anliggender har ventet med at give efter for Overmagtens *Tvang?*

Man kan ogsaa simplificere ved at stille Spørgsmaalet saaledes, om det var med den tyske Kniv paa Struben, at Erik Scavenius paa det danske Folks Vegne udtalte sin beundrende Forbavselse over Hitler-Tysklands Sejre, skrev under paa Antikomintern-Pagten, brød med Sovjetunionen og Kina, udleverede vore Torpedobaade, desarmerede to Trediedele af vor Hær, lod os plyndre for

The front page of an August 1943 issue of the Danish underground newspaper *Frit Danmark* (*Free Denmark*). Jørgen Kieler helped print and distribute the newspaper.

made at the beginning of the occupation was to limit freedom of the press. They wanted to control the news and ideas the Danes would hear. People like Kieler resisted the German domination of people's minds by printing what the Germans would not allow. *Frit Danmark* and other illegal papers ran stories of Allied victories and German defeats. They repeated the news that came from contacts in England and Sweden. The papers had cartoons that made fun of Germany.

With his brother, one of his sisters, and others, Kieler produced the newspapers in his apartment. Every week, they stuffed copies in mailboxes and left them in public places. The underground press kept up the spirits of freedom-loving Danes and irritated power-hungry Nazis.

Circulation of illegal papers was only one form of nonviolent resistance. Another was the *V Campaign*. "V" was the symbol for victory that English politician Winston Churchill had made popular. It was also the first letter in *vinde*, the Danish word for "win." During the occupation, Danes began using the letter V like a secret code. Radio broadcasts, newspaper headlines, and store advertisements used as many Vs as they could: "The letter began appearing wherever there was a blank space on an open wall . . . and Beethoven's Fifth Symphony became a favorite selection on the radio; it duplicated in musical terms the Morse code for the letter V—dot, dot, dash."[2]

The V Campaign was a way for Danes to silently defy the Germans. Another was to simply snub them. Danes gave German soldiers the "cold shoulder." They refused to speak to

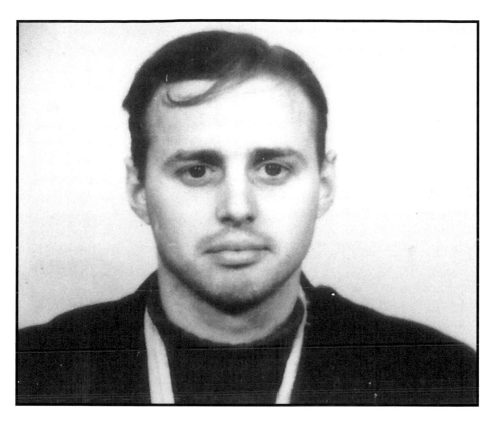

Jørgen Kieler was a member of the Danish resistance movement.

the Germans, walked out of stores when Germans walked in, and crossed to the other side of the street when they saw Germans coming. This quiet disdain annoyed the Germans, but it did not change anything. Kieler—and many others—wanted to do something to hurt the occupiers.

Frit Danmark and the other papers began suggesting more active forms of resistance. The press spoke directly to Danish workers. Germany used Danish labor for its war. German ships were being repaired in Denmark's shipyards. Denmark's factories produced rockets, airplane parts, and other materials that went to Germany. The underground papers encouraged Danes in these industries to sabotage their work. They did not have to do anything violent. They could merely work at a slower pace. Machinery could break down so production would stop. Repairs could take a long time. Orders could be misunderstood and parts lost. Employees could even go on strike, refusing to work.

Many readers did what the underground press suggested. These measures were effective, and the papers urged stronger actions. They described how to blow up factories that produced goods for Germany. These articles generated controversy throughout the underground. Kieler and his brother and sisters belonged to Holger Danske, one of the largest resistance groups. Some in the group were opposed to any violence, and others saw no other way to resist what they saw as evil. This issue divided Kieler's own family.

Resistance Fighter

The conflict brought Kieler to a critical decision: How could he ask people to risk capture, prison, and perhaps death while he simply printed articles? He could not. As a matter of conscience, Kieler became a saboteur. The point of his sabotage, however, was to resist, not to kill. He just wanted to cause the Germans enough problems to make them leave. He tried to make sure buildings were empty when he bombed them.

Other Danes had come to the same conclusion, but the vast majority remained passive. That is, until the Rosh Hashanah raid. The attempt to persecute the country's Jews did more to incite

Denmark to action than any other event. Kieler noted, "Now all those who were in favor of passive resistance were ready to prove that their morality was of the same quality as those who were willing to sacrifice their lives."[3] Overnight, thousands sprang to the aid of their fellow Danes. Kieler described the rescue of the Jews as both a united act of resistance and an expression of compassion:

> Many of us came from the organized resistance, but others came spontaneously when they were needed. National independence and democracy were our common goals, but the persecution of Jews added a new and overwhelming dimension to our fight against Hitler: human rights.[4]

Rescuer

Kieler explained how he became a rescuer: "It was necessary to find the dividing line between Good and Evil."[5] The way Kieler saw it, what the Germans were doing to the Jews was evil. Anything to stop it was good.

Kieler's part in the rescue was to get the Jews in Copenhagen to the fishing boats. His entire family was involved. Even before the raid, his father had helped two Czech Jews escape to Sweden. His sister was one of the two students who raised a million *kroner* for Ebba Lund's export operation. With no experience and no real plan, they all dove into the project:

> *We had to improvise everything: find hiding places, find boats, find money. . . . We had contacts with the fishermen, and we were able to hire their boats. In fact, the difficulty wasn't the money nor the boats; it was, at least at first, to make contacts with the Jews and to lead them to the embarkation points.[6]*

Once the word spread, Kieler found his job easy; so many people were eager to help. Years later, when some criticized the fishermen who charged money for their service, Kieler explained:

> *Certain ones belonged to the Resistance and wanted nothing. Others were frightened, in case they would be caught by the Germans, that they would confiscate their boats: they therefore wanted the ability to buy another one. . . . They forgot that if they were arrested the Germans would also confiscate their lives! Other fishermen [saw] an opportunity to make money. . . . But, all the fishermen, it is true, were in the front line for that evacuation.[7]*

The Kielers' inexperience did not hold them back. They and their group helped save the lives of nearly a thousand Jews.

Rescued

After the Jewish refugees were safely in Sweden, Kieler returned to the primary work of Holger Danske: sabotage. Eventually, he was caught. A kind Gestapo agent saved him, his father, his brother, and his two sisters from a firing squad and sent them to concentration camps instead.

Kieler slaved for six months in the Porta Westfalica camp in Germany. With little food or rest, he dug through hard rock. The prisoners built underground factories that would withstand Allied bombs. Kieler sustained many injuries, including a fractured skull:

> I was beaten and stoned (yes, with stones!) with a friend because we were not working hard enough for the camp. My friend died. The doctor, who picked me up in a pitiable state, not only cared for me, but, learning that I was a medical student, gave orders for me to work with him from then on; that's what saved my life![8]

The Swedish Count Folke Bernadotte also saved his life. Kieler was one of the 15,000 concentration camp prisoners who rode the white buses to freedom. The resistance fighter who had risked his life to rescue others was himself among the rescued.

After the war, Kieler became a doctor. For many years, he directed the Danish Cancer Research Institute and served as

This is a freedom fighter armband from Denmark. After the Danish Jews were safely in Sweden, Danish resisters continued to sabotage and fight the Nazis.

president of the Danish Freedom Foundation. He studied and wrote about the post-traumatic stress disorder he called "Concentration Camp Syndrome."

For as long as he lives, Kieler will bear the physical and emotional scars of his experience in the resistance. But those negatives are far outweighed by the knowledge that he did what he believed was right. Denmark did what was right. "We must discover . . . the positive side of those years," he said. "The positive . . . is when someone takes the risk of sacrificing himself so that others may live."[9]

Georg Duckwitz, Karl Køster, Niels Bohr, Ebba Lund, Erling Kiær, Folke Bernadotte, Jørgen Kieler, and hundreds of ordinary Danes did the positive thing. They risked their lives so that eight thousand Jews could live.

Many Danes gather at the synagogue in Copenhagen on October 28, 2003, marking the sixtieth anniversary of the rescue of the Danish Jews.

Timeline

1940

April 9—Germany invades and occupies Denmark.

1941

November 25—Under intense German pressure, Denmark signs the Anti-Comintern Pact.

1942

September 26—King Christian X angers Hitler by his response to Hitler's birthday telegram.

November 5—Werner Best arrives in Copenhagen as the German plenipotentiary of Denmark.

1943

August—In August Uprising, Danish workers strike in seventeen cities; number of sabotage acts rises sharply.

August 24—Resistance group Holger Danske blows up the Forum.

August 28—Werner Best gives Danish government an ultimatum. Rather than meet Germany's conditions, Danish government resigns.

August 29—General von Hanneken imposes martial law in Denmark and places King Christian X under house arrest.

September 11—Werner Best tells Georg Duckwitz of plan to transport Danish Jews to Nazi camps.

September 17—German security police break into offices of Jewish Community Center and take records of names and addresses of Jews.

September 28—Duckwitz warns Hans Hedtoft of German plan to arrest Jews on October 1.

September 29—Rabbi Melchior tells Copenhagen congregation of German plans for deportation of Denmark's Jews.

September 30—Niels Bohr arrives safely in Sweden, petitions Swedish government to give refuge to Denmark's Jews.

October 1—Gestapo and Danish Nazis attempt unsuccessfully to arrest Denmark's Jews.

October—Danish people help 7,200 Jews and 700 non-Jewish relatives escape to Sweden.

October 9—Fourteen hundred Jews arrive in Sweden from Denmark, the greatest number on any one day.

1944

June 6—D-Day—Allies invade beaches of Normandy; Danish saboteurs blow up Globus factory outside Copenhagen.

June—Danish resistance commits many acts of sabotage and Danish workers strike in many Danish cities.

September 19—Germans arrest the Danish police and deport two thousand Danes to concentration camps.

1945

April—Swedish Red Cross brings Scandinavian and other prisoners, including Danes, from concentration camps in Germany to Sweden on White Buses.

April 15—White Buses take Danish Jews from Theresienstadt to Denmark, then Sweden.

April 23—Heinrich Himmler asks Count Folke Bernadotte to communicate his offer of conditional surrender of Germany's troops to Allied command. The offer is rejected.

April 30—Hitler commits suicide.

May 4—German forces in Denmark, Holland, and northwest Germany surrender.

May 8—Germany surrenders unconditionally, ending the war in Europe.

May—Danish Jews in Sweden return to Denmark.

Chapter Notes

Introduction Denmark Is Different

1. Bent Melchior, cited in Ronen Bodoni, "Jewish World," *Ynet News*, May 3, 2006, <http://www.ynetnews.com/articles/0,7340,L-3246548,00.html> (March 10, 2009).
2. Ibid.
3. In 1814, a law was passed that made all racial and religious discrimination in Denmark punishable.
4. Preben Munch-Nielsen, United States Holocaust Memorial Museum, *Holocaust Encyclopedia*, n.d., <http://www.ushmm.org/lcmedia/viewer/wlc/idcard.php?RefId=1652W> (June 28, 2008).
5. Niels Bamberger, *Interview*, United States Holocaust Memorial Museum, 1989, <http://www.ushmm.org/lcmedia/viewer/wlc/testimony.php?RefId=NBD0447M> (June 28, 2008).

Chapter 1 Sounding the Alarm: Georg Ferdinand Duckwitz

1. Cited in Leni Yahil, *The Rescue of Danish Jewry: Test of a Democracy* (Philadelphia: Jewish Publication Society of America, 1969), pp. 138–139.
2. From Duckwitz's memoirs, cited in Emmy E. Werner, *A Conspiracy of Decency* (Boulder, Colo.: Westview, 2002), p. 37.
3. Hans Hedtoft, foreword to *October '43*, by Aage Bertelsen (Munich: Ner Tamid Verlag, 1960), pp. 13–14.

4. On the night of October 1–2, a total of 284 were arrested, but some were released. Only 202 were transported to Theresienstadt.

Chapter 2 Hiding Strangers: Dr. Karl Henrik Køster

1. Cited in Harold Flender, *Rescue in Denmark* (New York: Simon and Schuster, 1963), p. 124. All information on Dr. Køster is from Dr. Køster's personal statements to Flender corroborated by others.
2. Robert Pedersen, cited in Herbert Pundik, *In Denmark It Could Not Happen: The Flight of the Jews to Sweden in 1943* (Jerusalem: Gefen, 1998), p. 28.
3. Flender, p. 124.
4. Cited in Peter Ackerman and Jack Duvall, *A Force More Powerful: A Century of Nonviolent Conflict* (New York: Macmillan, 2000), p. 215.
5. Knud Pedersen, *Churchill-Klubben* (Copenhagen: Bogens, 1945, 1991).
6. Ibid.
7. Flender, p. 123.
8. Ibid., p. 124.

Chapter 3 Finding a Safe Place: Niels Bohr

1. Nobel Laureates, University of Copenhagen, n.d., <http://www.ku.dk/english/introduction/?content=http://www.ku.dk/english/introduction/nobel_laureates.htm> (July 5, 2008).
2. Niels Bohr Archive, Document 6: Draft Document in Margarethe Bohr's Handwriting, Documents Relating to 1941 Bohr-Heisenberg Meeting, released February 6, 2002, <http://www.nba.nbi.dk/papers/docs/d06tra.htm> (July 5, 2008).

3. Ibid.

4. Ibid.

5. Cited in Thomas Powers, *Heisenberg's War: The Secret History of the German Bomb* (New York: Alfred A. Knopf, 1993), p. 231.

6. Ibid., pp. 239–240.

7. Niels Bohr, Open Letter to the United Nations, June 9, 1950, printed in *Impact of Science on Society*, vol. 1, no. 2, 1950, p. 68.

8. Ibid.

Chapter 4 **From the City to the Sea: Ebba Lund**

1. Quoted in Donald H. Harrison, "'Girl in Red Cap' Saved Hundreds of Jews," *San Diego Jewish Press-Heritage*, January 14, 1994, <http://www.jewishsightseeing.com/denmark/copenhagen/1994-01-14_red_cap_girl.htm> (July 1, 2008).

2. Ibid.

3. Ibid.

4. Ibid.

5. Elsebeth Kieler, quoted in Herbert Pundik, *In Denmark It Could Not Happen: The Flight of the Jews to Sweden in 1943* (Jerusalem: Gefen, 1998), pp. 107–108.

6. Ole Lippman, a leader of the resistance, cited in Harold Flender, *Rescue in Denmark: How Occupied Denmark Rose as a Nation to Save the Danish Jews from Nazi Extermination* (New York: Simon and Schuster, 1963), pp. 224–225.

7. Børge Outze, ed., *Denmark During the German Occupation* (Copenhagen: Scandinavian Publishing Company, 1946), cited in Flender, p. 229.

8. Harrison.

9. Ibid.

10. Ibid.

Chapter 5 From Denmark to Sweden: Erling Kiær

1. Niels Sørensen, quoted in Marek Halter, *Stories of Deliverance: Speaking with Men and Women Who Rescued Jews from the Holocaust*, trans. Michael Bernard (Chicago: Open Court, 1998).
2. Preben Munch-Nielsen, U.S. Holocaust Memorial Museum interview, 1989, <http://www.ushmm.org/lcmedia/viewer/wlc/testimony.php?RefId=PNB0300M> (July 1, 2008).
3. Ulrich Plesner, letter, *Jerusalem Post*, January 30, 1979.
4. Erling Kiaer, *Med Gestapo i Kølvandet* (*With the Gestapo in Pursuit*), not translated into English, (Copenhagen: Frimodts Forlag, 1946), p. 77.
5. Ibid.

Chapter 6 Saved! Leo Goldberger

1. Leo Goldberger, in C. Rittner and S. Myers, eds., *Courage to Care: Rescuers of Jews During the Holocaust* (New York: New York University Press, 1986), p. 92.
2. Ibid., p. 95.
3. Leif Donde, U.S. Holocaust Memorial Museum interview, 1989, <http://www.ushmm.org/lcmedia/viewer/wlc/testimony.php?RefId=LDE0326M> (July 1, 2008).
4. Goldberger, p. 94.

Chapter 7 Captured: Birgit Krasnik Fischermann

1. Birgit Krasnik Fischermann, *Active Fredsreiser*, translated from Norwegian, n.d., <http://translate.google.com/translate?hl=en&sl=no&u=http://www.aktive-fredsreiser.no/administrasjon/tidsvitne_birgit_krasnik_fischermann.htm&sa=X&oi=translate

&resnum=6&ct=result&prev=/search%3Fq%3DBirgit%
2BKrasnik%2BFischermann%26hl%3Den%26rls%3DDMUS,
DMUS:2006-32,DMUS:en> (July 22, 2008).

2. Ibid.

3. Ibid.

4. Cited in Harold Flender, *Rescue in Denmark: How Occupied Denmark Rose as a Nation to Save the Danish Jews from Nazi Extermination* (New York: Simon and Schuster, 1963), p. 64.

5. Krasnik Fischermann.

6. Birgit Krasnik Fischermann, in *Kristeligt Dagblad*, translated from Danish, June 20, 2007, <http://translate.google.com/ translate?hl=en&sl=da&u=http://www.kristeligt-dagblad.dk/ artikel/254780:Historie--Bedraget-i-byen-bag-tremmer%3Fhighl ight%3Ddagblad&sa=X&oi=translate&resnum=10&ct=resul t&prev=/search%3Fq%3DBirgit%2BKrasnik%2BFischermann %26hl%3Den%26rls%3DDMUS,DMUS:2006-32,DMUS:en> (July 25, 2008).

7. Hana Mueller, *Theresienstadt*, Unites States Holocaust Memorial Museum, n.d., <http://www.ushmm.org/wlc/media_ oi.php?lang=en&ModuleId=10005424&MediaId=1766> (May 23, 2008).

Chapter 8 Sweden Helps: Count Folke Bernadotte

1. Tove Schoenbaum Bamberger, United States Holocaust Memorial Museum, 1989 interview, <http://www.ushmm. org/lcmedia/viewer/wlc/testimony.php?RefId=TBE0448F> (May 23, 2008).

2. Ibid.

3. Folke Bernadotte, *The Curtain Falls: Last Days of the Third Reich*, trans. Eric Lewenhaupt (New York: A. A. Knopf, 1945), p. 16.

4. Ibid., p. 21.

5. Rabbi Marcus Melchior, cited in Harold Flender, *Rescue in Denmark: How Occupied Denmark Rose as a Nation to Save the Danish Jews from Nazi Extermination* (New York: Simon and Schuster, 1963), p. 254.

Chapter 9 From Rescuer to Rescued: Jørgen Kieler

1. Jørgen Kieler, June 21, 2000, cited in Angela Brink, Stephen Kang, and Lillian Marsh, "In Search of Humanity in Action," 2000, <http://www.humanityinaction.org/docs/LIbrary/2000% 20Extracted/ Brink,_Kang__Marsh_2000.pdf> (August 9, 2008).

2. Richard Petrow, *The Bitter Years: The Invasion and Occupation of Denmark and Norway, April 1940–May 1945* (New York: William Morrow and Company, 1974), p. 170.

3. Jørgen Kieler, cited in Michael Berenbaum, *The World Must Know: The History of the Holocaust as Told in the United States Holocaust Memorial Museum*, second edition (Washington, D.C.: United States Holocaust Memorial Museum, 1993), pp. 159–160.

4. Ibid., p. 161.

5. Cited in Marek Halter, *Stories of Deliverance: Speaking with Men and Women Who Rescued Jews from the Holocaust*, trans. Michael Bernard (La Salle, Ill.: Open Court Publishing, 1998), p. 130.

6. Ibid., p. 129.

7. Ibid.

8. Ibid., p. 131.

9. Ibid., pp. 130–131.

Glossary

Aktion   German for "action." Used by Nazis for any type of operation against Jews, usually a raid, or roundup.

Allies   The collection of nations allied, or joined together, against Germany, Italy, and Japan in World War II. More than forty countries made up the Allies, many joining late in the war. The main Allies were the United Kingdom (which includes England), the United States, the Soviet Union, France, Canada, Australia, and China.

attaché   A person who is a diplomat of one country, usually a technical expert, working for that country in another country.

bookbinder   A person who glues pages together to form books.

cantor   A person who sings during ceremonies and observances at Jewish synagogues.

convoy   Group of vehicles carrying soldiers or military supplies.

Gestapo   Literally, the _Geheime Staatspolizei_, the Nazi State Secret Police.

hull   Main body of a ship.

krone (plural: *kroner*)   Literally "crown," Danish unit of money.
              In 1943, five *kroner* were worth about one dollar.

mediator   A person who helps two people or groups who have a
              disagreement to come to a settlement.

Øresund   The sound, or narrow body of water, that separates
              Denmark from Sweden.

plenipotentiary   Literally "full" (pleni) "power" (potent), refers
              to a diplomat with full power to represent his or
              her country in doing official business with another
              country.

protectorate   A country or region under the protection of another
              country.

sabotage   Act of deliberately damaging goods or plans of
              someone else, usually in secret.

saboteur   One who commits acts of sabotage.

sanctuary   A place of refuge, or protection.

Scandinavia   A region of northern Europe that encompasses
              Denmark, Norway, and Sweden and sometimes
              Finland and Iceland.

sound   A narrow body of water connecting larger bodies of water.

synagogue   Jewish house of worship.

underground   Illegal—done under the surface of the ground, or in secret.

Further Reading

Boraks-Nemetz, Lilian, and Irene N. Watts, eds. *Tapestry of Hope: Holocaust Writing for Young People*. Plattsburg, N.Y.: Tundra Books of Northern New York, 2003.

Goldberger, Leo, ed. *Rescue of the Danish Jews: Moral Courage Under Stress*. New York: New York University Press, 1987.

Kieler, Jørgen, translated by Eric Dickens. *Resistance Fighter*. New York: Gefen Publishing House, 2008.

Levine, Ellen. *Darkness Over Denmark: The Danish Resistance and the Rescue of the Jews*. New York: Holiday House, 2000.

Smith, Lyn. *Remembering: Voices of the Holocaust: A New History in the Words of the Men and Women Who Survived*. New York: Basic Books, 2007.

Toksvig, Sandi. *Hitler's Canary*. New York: Roaring Brook Press, 2007.

Zapruder, Alexandra, ed. *Salvaged Pages: Young Writers' Diaries of the Holocaust*. New Haven, Conn.: Yale University Press, 2002.

Internet Addresses

Jewish Virtual Library:

The Virtual Jewish History Tour—Denmark

< http://www.jewishvirtuallibrary.org/jsource/vjw/Denmark.html >

United States Holocaust Memorial Museum:

The Rescue of the Jews of Denmark

< http://www.ushmm.org/museum/exhibit/focus/danish/ >

Yad Vashem:

The Holocaust Martyrs' and Heroes' Remembrance Authority

< http://www.yadvashem.org/ >

Index